CW00854613

Leca Diaries:

Grounded ramblings of a flying doctor

Dr Andrew Nicholas William Evans

The first of many diaries I hope, Merry Christmas you old fart.

Nick

Entry...	page

It rained all day yesterday and was rather cold. We were lazy and stayed home.
This morning was glorious, blue sky, warm sun, cool breeze. So after a breakfast of
fried tomato and mushrooms (me), porridge and fruit (Linda) we set off at 09.40 to
walk up the track towards Le Faig. The rain had brought out the slugs and gorgeous
red-brown fungi. The footprints of the izard showed in the mud. The first primroses
on the bank. A whole variety of flowers blooming. Butterflies - orange tips, clouded
yellows, peacocks, blues, whites, fritillaries.
We passed Can Robert, Las Cassase, Mas de Léca, with crumbling terracing up above
us on the hillside, the remains of stone built ramps and stairs leading up the slope
from when the slopes were cleared of trees and cultivated.
Finally we reached Tourre d'en Glas, a small house with open shutters and curtains
but no sign of occupation. There were large, attached, ruined farm buildings, a crane,
a digger, an abandoned jeep, and signs of building repairs uncompleted. I know that
there was a young man living there last year. I suppose he is self isolating elsewhere.
I hope he will return to complete the work.
This was 2.8k from our house. I turned back at this point. The descent is
uncomfortable on my knees but getting better with each time I go up the hill.
In the afternoon it was my turn to prepare supper. It was not a great success. I tried a
new chicken curry recipe. It involved dry roasting yellow mustard and sesame seeds. I
roasted them in a dry frying pan. When they were done I took them off the heat and
left them in the pan to cool. I guess that's when they burned. It gave a bitter taste to
the sauce. I added a spoon full of sugar which dulled the bitterness, but not enough
for my dinner guest. I also burned the potato and cauliflower, and over cooked the
onion bhajis. So, all in all a total f**k up.

How was your day.

The Butcher of Arles

It's a cold grey day threatening rain, a good enough excuse in my book, for avoiding a soaking on a 5k yomp and staying in writing and painting. Here is Emily, who is my son Nick's goddaughter:

Living next door to Michèle has it's advantages. Her man is Roger who is the 'Butcher of Arles' (this should be said slowly, basso profundo with a haunted expression for full effect.) He is, of course, not a mass murderer, well not as far as I know, but what do I know? He is a charming man though for me conversation with him is next to impossible because of his very strong Catalan accent. Be that as it may, he is a butcher, he is working, he has meat and, like all good Frenchmen, he comes home for lunch. We can therefore ask Michèle in the morning, by FB messaging of course, for an order of meat. She gives Roger the order at lunch time and he comes back with the meat in the evening. Perfecto.

So yesterday we took delivery of 3kg minced beef, 8 chick joints and 4 lamb leg steaks. When Michèle brought the order to our door she asked if we would like some sanglier (wild boar). 'Well,' we said, 'is the bear catholic?' So 5min later she was back with two plastic bags of meat from her freezer, mostly sanglier but also one pack of izard. As some of you will know, the 'chasse' is very popular round here, many sanglier and other creatures and a few hunters are shot! The meat cannot be sold because it hasn't been inspected by a vet, slaughtered in an abattoir and passed for human consumption, which is a problem because I was human when I last checked. There is a possibility that the meat may be contaminated with parasites. The solution to this is to keep the meat in the freezer for three months, then cook the hell out of it with lots of red wine, herbs and spices. Which is what my resident chef is now busy doing

I apologise to any vegetarians and other sensitive souls. I am looking forward to a Daube de Sanglier à la Michel Roux Jr. and a terrine - à recipe in 'Marie-Claire'. Then there's the izard to deal with. Any suggestions? Is there no end to Linda's talents ? Cook extraordinaire, travel agent supreme, wife, mother, grandmother, lover...the list goes on. And gardener. We have potatoes in pots. She planted cut up chunks of sprouting manky spuds and they have emerged as vigorous plants. French beans, some old seed beans which she planted and thought had been killed off by recent snow but have started to emerge. Tomato seeds and coriander seeds are beginning to germinate in flat trays which I spray with water every few hours and bring in at night.

The garden centres were mostly shut except for some selling pet food, but they have started to open again so Linda went down this morning, this time remembering her attestation, to buy some begonias, geraniums and chilli peppers. So that is her next job after the meat.

I hope you are all well, keeping fit, not murdering each other, enjoying the simple things. If you wish to stop receiving these emails, you might want to speak to the serial killer next door.

And, as the waiting staff in restaurants (remember them?) say as they deliver something you didn't order, 'Enjoy!' (Don't you just want to strangle them?)
Er, I think my medication is wearing off......Andrew

Cellar Raiding   21/04/20

Greetings Earthlings,

I imagine this must be what it's like on a Space Station. Linda has just set off on a 'spacewalk' to Intermarché, though obviously she's taken the car (or moon buggy as I like to think of it). Last time she went shopping two weeks ago, driving back through Amélie she saw a man returning from shopping, with his face mask protecting his chin and a fag in his mouth.

I understand that those of you in the UK have been enjoying some glorious weather. Well, bully for you. If you watch the weather forecast, there is a point half way through when a map of Western Europe appears. At the moment the UK is sitting under high pressure which is not moving. Well, let me tell you, that high is being kept in place by a huge swirl of sodden air which is dumping millions of gallons of rain on the rest of the civilised world. And Andorra.

On Saturday we walked up the road to Mas Cazenove. Tony and Lucy are locked down (iPad wanted 'locked up', what do they know ?) in SE London so we offered to go and check that all was well, that was the ostensible reason for going, but in truth our main objective was to boost our dwindling stocks of cava by raiding the cellar. As we are so isolated I decided as we were leaving the house that we didn't need to bother with attestations. On the way, and well beyond 1k from the house, Antoine, the mayor drove up behind us and stopped for a brief, socially distant chat.

We got up to the Mas. The gutter that drains the constant gushing water across the top of the drive was partly blocked with a mixture of sticks, leaves and mud. I watched in awe as my wife went down on her hands and knees and cleared the blockage. Such dexterity, such grace. I'd have helped, but my knees...

We opened up the ground floor shutters to give the house some air. There was sunshine that day. There were four bottles of cava.

We set off to walk back which is down hill so sore on my knees. There was almost no traffic. A couple of cars parked up by people sneaking off up into the mountains. Then, round the corner heading up hill towards us came a police car. We, of course, didn't have attestations - my fault as was rapidly pointed out- but fortunately the car cruised on past us without pause. There aren't many properties further up the hill so it was difficult to imagine where they were going. Possibly to the 'rainbow' camp. The farm have lost two more sheep to a couple of unknown dogs.

Whilst Linda was trying to fill in an attestation on her phone another vehicle appeared. This was a Mountain Rescue 4x4, they slowed as if to inspect us, decided we weren't their quarry and drove on. It was a relief to realise that the two vehicles were almost certainly heading up to find/rescue/arrest someone who wasn't obeying the rules.

On Sunday it drizzled most of the day so we stayed in, wimps that we are.

On Monday, yesterday, rain was forecast but didn't materialise, the clouds lifted, so we set off to walk up the track. Linda rapidly spotted two slugs and declared that there were 'lots of' slugs. There then followed a profound debate about the difference between 'a few', 'quite a few' and 'a lot' when discussing slugs. I felt that we needed to see at least 15 to be able to say that there were 'a lot'. When we had counted 20 slugs (definitely 'a lot'), I turned back leaving linda to carry on further up, listening to her audio book. Have others found that isolation makes you bonkers, or is it just me?

Today it is raining stair rods, so I don't think we'll be walking. I'm going to tackle a biryani again.

Good health

Andrew

Dettol Injections   24/04/20

Thankyou for the (mostly positive) feedback. Nothing much to report. We've had a lot of rain so our river is high and loud.

Sheila, who runs the watercolour group in Céret, has continued very enthusiastically on line. She introduced us to Galina Shargina, a St. Petersburg artist and has had us painting flowers. My effort is based on a photo posted on Facebook by Jacqueline Dauphin.

Just off to have my Detol injection as advised by Prof. Trump. I'm then thinking that , if I survive the injection, I might try shoving a UV lamp up where the sun don't shine. Should be able to get a paper in the Lancet out of this.

Remember, friends, alternative treatments should always be preferred to anything that has actually been tested.

Andrew

Isolation art challenge   28/04/20

The days are beginning to drag just a teeny weeny bit.

The 23rd was, of course, St.George's Day. Or if you prefer, Shakespeare's birthday. And apparently also his death day. Which is a bit weird. It also happens to be our wedding anniversary. We decided to go out to a restaurant with a few friends, maybe take in a show, and round it all off in a nightclub. But then we thought, what the heck, let's just stay in. So that's what we did.

The 26th was Linda's birthday which started with the Australian granddaughters singing 'Happy Birthday' on FaceTime. Well, the wedding anniversary celebration went so well we decided to do it again for the birthday. The difference was that I did the cooking. Well actually I heated up the daube de sanglier which someone made the other day.

Before supper we had virtual apéro with friends in Reynès, there was champagne, and pâté de foie gras on toast.

A few days ago, our son, Nick, and his flat mate, Jack, went to Jack's parents to move a heavy pot plant out of the house. They then went to our house, hoping to borrow some outdoor cushions as they are spending a lot of time in the back garden. Looking through the French windows, they saw a pigeon in the sitting room. It had come down the chimney. Presumably unable to remember how it got in, and becoming distressed at finding itself trapped, it proceeded to leave its mark on the furniture and the windows. Nick released the bird, and cleaned up the mess. There can surely be nothing more that you can ask of your son than he clean pigeon shit off your settee.

Saw this plant yesterday, is it a vetch?

In a recent message I showed my painting of flowers. I have joined a Facebook site called 'The Isolation Art Challenge' which invites you to post art work. There is a list of proposed daily themes. I started to do this, drawing some cartoons but couldn't keep up with daily posts. So after a pause of a week or so, and the day after President Trump made his extraordinary comments about potential covid treatments, I decided to post my flowers, introducing them thus: 'Day- who knows? Glad to report that the dettol injections are working and when I can get this uv lamp up inside I'll be fine.'

The response has been astonishing. There have been over 380 'likes' from all round the world. There have been some, mostly complementary or humorous, comments, and one Canadian woman who gently berated me, saying that Trump was only joking. Feeling rather smug about the large number of 'likes' I was idly scanning through some Facebook profiles, only to find that one of my 'likers' is what we Brits would call 'Far Right', but in Middle America is probably run of the mill, middle of the road. She was pro Trump (I can only assume she didn't read my introductory remarks and just looked at the painting), virulently anti Obama, pro gun, anti abortion, and ferociously anti 'Socialism'. Ah well, takes all sorts.

Yesterday was warm with high thin clouds. We walked up the track. I managed 3.1k before turning back. Mrs Evans, who seems to becoming rather fit, went on to 5.7k before turning back.

Raining today, housework and cooking. Now have Prime Minister Philippe on the TV. He's talking about easing the lock down. It seems it's going to vary from one region to another.

Gradual reopening schools from 11may. Shops reopening but not bars or restaurants. He is advocating the wearing of masks.

I see that Trish Greenhalgh, Prof of General Practice in Oxford has published an article which seems to demonstrate that cloth masks radically reduced virus transmission by infected people. So I may have to review my opinion.

Stay safe, cough into your oxter, wear a mask in bed. We will survive!
Andrew

Apres Shampoo

Good grief, it's May already.

Things that have been cancelled : Wimbledon, the Boat Race, football, rugby, the Olympics, the Lib. Dem. Spring Conference, the Sanch in Perpignan, Céret Feria, Fête des Cerise, Mayoral Elections, the list is endless. Will the Eurovision Song Contest survive?

I'm beginning to find this lock down oppressive. I want to just get in the car and drive somewhere, go across the border for lunch, go to a beach for a paddle, sit in a bar with un demi, eat in a restaurant, go shopping with my wife so I can get the things she doesn't think we need, hug female acquaintances for just half a second too long...

But for now I must be content with walking up the track till my lungs burst and my muscles give up, then lying on the sofa reading.

I find that I'm observing the world around me intensely. I see the profusion and variety of wild flowers and other plants, brown millipedes, butterflies, caterpillars, and two dead shrews on the path. Looking south to the crest and the Spanish border, I see eagles circling on the thermals then heading north on their summer migration. The track verges are dug up by sanglier rooting for tasty morsels. We never see them but there are lots of them hiding in the dense undergrowth waiting for dusk. New

growth pine needles are the most intense bright green.

One of the problems in life is having to take your glasses off when you take a shower so that it's difficult to know which bottle is which. For some days now I've been puzzled by the shampoo which doesn't seem to lather like it should. We, of course, have bathroom products labelled in various languages. The bottle label said 'Shampooing', but today I turned the bottle slightly to the left, held it up to the light, squinted, and read the word 'Après' to the left of the word 'Shampooing'. I haven't told Mrs. Evans so keep it to yourselves.

I see that Scotland, where I spent seven happy years, has just repealed it's Blasphemy Law and replaced it with a law which prevents you from criticising Islam, Trans people etc but don't worry lads, you can continue to say what you like about the fair sex because they aren't an oppressed minority.

Well, though this is the Léca Diaries, I don't seem to have told you about the news from Léca. Contain yourselves, it'll have to keep for another day.

Greetings. Suddenly we have a reminder that summer is on the way. It's hot. Get the sun cream out for the first time this year (question : when did sun tan cream and bronzing cream become sun screen f50?).

Breaking news.
'Yucatan Life' informs us that the closure of liquor stores imposed with the lockdown, designed to discourage tourism and domestic violence, is to be extended for the time being. The unintended consequences include a dramatic increase in liquor store burglary, an increase in domestic violence committed by what they describe as 'clinical alcoholics', and a booming black market in beer and tequila. Thankfully, in France, it is still possible to get your medication from Intermarché - other outlets are available.

Today we broke the rules. Up till now we have confined ourselves to walking from the house up the track towards Le Faig. We have exceeded the 1k rule and not bothered with attestations but we only ever see Johan with his dogs, or Françoise with a couple of her foster children so no problem.

Today we got in the car. Both of us. TOGETHER. And drove up to Col de la Descarga and walked to the Tour de Batère. We'll probably be dragged away in chains, but we don't care. It was worth it.
When we parked the car the sky was clear, and so blue, and the sun was hot. There was no-one else. Silence appart from birdsong, rushing water, and the intermittent far away thump of a diesel generator. The flash of colour from a small tortoise shell butterfly. After the recent rain, the little streams which are often no more than a trickle, are now alive with rushing, tumbling water, their banks adorned with marsh marigolds and cowslips. Fungi have erupted. There are puddles full of tadpoles. Ravens fly overhead with their harsh deep call. A

blackcap sings in a tree. Snow still lingers on the tops but we are bathed in warm sunshine.

As we came to the tower we heard a buzzing overhead. We looked up. Something in the sky circling over us.... is it a bird ? Is it a plane? Well it clearly isn't Superman! It's a DRONE. We've been spotted. The gendarmes are ready to pounce! We continued round the tower, half expecting a megaphone voice to shout orders at us from the sky. On the grass by the path there was a camper van with its concertina roof up, and two 'directors' chairs. A young man in trousers and sandals was packing away his drone. Eventually a woman in T-shirt and harem pants emerged from the van.

We returned the way we came leaving the couple to their idyll. The horses which were in Corsavy a couple of weeks ago are now up at the Col. They were hanging around our car when we returned to it.

In other news from Léca.

Charlène is with child, and is locked down with her man in her parents' house. The boyfriend and Charlène's father are creating a vegetable garden by clearing a bit of terraced land below Can Robert. Last time this was tried some years ago by Johan and his father they fought a loosing battle with marauding sanglier. So good luck I say. Garlic and Laure in the school house have started to develop the old orchard into a vegetable garden. They have put up a greenhouse, and made a plot for a variety of vegetables.

They also built an enclosed chicken run against the wall below the road. The wire fence was buried into the ground to prevent the foxes from burrowing underneath. They bought two hens, and we started chucking our scraps over the wall. The hens started laying. The children had their first fresh eggs. Then yesterday morning, no

chickens. Mr Fox came in the night, jumped down off the wall and had chicken dinner.

It's 'Peyton Place' meets 'Clochmerle' here.

I think it's going to be impossible to go shopping without a mask.

Hasta la vista baby

Stay safe, stay sober (I'm KIDDING)   08/05/20

Greetings. Hot sunny day. Stiff breeze.

Can't remember the last time I saw a vapour trail overhead.

Prime Minister Philippe and members of his cabinet appeared on TV yesterday afternoon to announce changes to the lockdown. France is divided into two. The green zone which is the west and south has lower numbers of cases, and the red north and east sector including Paris is the red zone. In the green zone from Monday, primarily schools will start to open on a voluntary basis with reduced class sizes. Older children will return later. Public transport will be increased. People will return to work with social distancing (sd). We can travel up to 100k within our Department (though there are various interpretations of this rule) without an attestation. But as bars, restaurants, beaches and the Spanish border remain closed, the only difference that will make to us is that we can go to Auchan and 5Continents in Perpignan. It'll be interesting to see what Boris has to say on Sunday. One thing's for sure, he'll have to put up with much more ferocious press questioning than the French ministers get.

Yesterday I had an appointment at the Clinique in Céret with the cardiologue. So I set off with my attestation, passport and mask. The mask was made by our neighbour, Michèle, who is making them for the local care home. Amélie market was open. How can they do sd? Walking back from the market was a bearded lady. A long white mane of hair down her back and a white beard on her chin. Except, of course it was her mask.

L. S. Lowry did a portrait of a bearded lady he claimed to have seen on a bus in Manchester. I think he just did it to wind up his mother.

Alan Emery was Prof. of Medical Genetics in Edinburgh. He was also an artist. When he was a student at Sheffield Medical School he was secretary of the Art Soc. One day Lowry came to give a talk. Alan had a car and so was tasked with taking the guest speaker home. When they arrived, Lowry invited him in for a cup of tea. Alan was left in the living room and, seeing a stack of canvases against a wall, went to take a look. Lowry returned with the tea and said, ' Do you like them ?'. (All this must be said in a genteel Manchester accent.) Alan replied in the affirmative. Lowry said, 'You can have one if you like.' Alan, bashful, polite, nervous, said, 'Oh no Mr Lowry, I couldn't.' ...to his eternal regret.

Arriving at the clinic I donned my new mask for the first time. The elastic loops were a bit short so my ears were pulled outwards making me look like Alfred E Neuman of Mad Magazine.

I approached the doors which normally slide open. But not today. A clerk opened the door and asked me my business. She checked her list, took my temperature and gave me a squirt of hand sanitizer. She took me to a waiting room with one chair in each corner. I got the one by the door so everyone coming in or out brushed past my knees.

My cardiologue is one of those irritatingly thin fit people who asks you about your weight. He is Spanish, well, no, Catalan. With a Russian father. He trained in Stockholm. And works in France. He tells me his Swedish is a bit rusty. Oh, did I say that he speaks a bit of English which helps when my French gives up.

After the echo and examination we sat at his desk and he yanked off his mask muttering darkly about the discomfort, and invited me to do likewise.

Heart ok, BP ok, weight down! Come back in 3 months.

Well, that's the most excitement I'll have for a while. Hope you're all having as much fun.

Thanks Tony for your avocado based comments, and to Jonathan for an epic response.

Enjoyed some opera from Nancy, and exercise recommendations from Wally. Jon continues to entertain on Facebook with an amazingly eclectic song book. (Not entirely sure what eclectic means but I think I've got away with it.) Doug has offered me the rules of cricket which he seems to think will help me to understand lockdown. My sister in Bath tells me she's living next door to James Brown, but he's had recent heart surgery, so is presumably not a Sex Machine.

Stay safe, stay sober (I'm KIDDING)

Groundhog Day   11/05/20

I've had a complaint that I haven't posted a diary entry for a while, though the last entry was on the 8th.
I'm finding life a bit groundhoggy.
Get up (late), check weight on bathroom scales after business and before cup of tea , discuss breakfast, make breakfast, eat breakfast. I like my porridge with water and salt, Linda likes hers with milk and prunes. Decide to go for a walk. It rains. Abandon walk. Read emails, Facebook, Twitter. Discuss lunch. Do exercise video for 20 mins (me, sometimes). Prep lunch, eat it. Discuss supper. Decide who's going to make supper. Read a book. It's stopped raining. Go for a walk. It starts raining again. Return home. Think about doing a painting. Put it off. Prepare apéro. Watch Government Briefing. Shout at journalists. And it's 6pm! (Only 5 pm in UK) Have a drink. Eat the nibbles whilst waiting for our virtual drinks guests. Have another drink. Talk to friends. Make supper, which may include burning the leeks. Watch reruns on TV. Go to bed.
There are of course some variations. We have had some good walks in fine weather. Sometimes I don't burn the leeks. We may have a third drink. Ok, we always have a third.

When Linda went shopping last week in Intermarché, you could only buy three of any item. So she loaded up the trolley with fruit, vegetables, meat, etc, and a box of red wine (well, two boxes), three bottles of blanquette de Limoux, and three of crémant de Bourgogne, there being no cava to be had. At the checkout, the woman behind her in the queue asked if she was buying the fizz to celebrate when easing of the lockdown started. Linda replied, ' No, that's just to see me through till till the lockdown is eased'.
Today there has been the beginnings of easing of lockdown. We were able to go out together in the car for up to 100k (or 60miles as the Today Program had it) from our house. So we drove down to Amélie to order printer cartridges and book a Control Technique which we thought was due in June, but was actually due in March.
There are some shops open in Amélie. Street markets are restarting. And the beautician is open. This is obviously an enormous relief to some of us. But as yet no hairdressers.
This no coiffure thing is clearly a big problem. Kate Silverton's is a right mess. An as for Thomasz Schafernaker, well, a disaster. I'm ok with my clippers but Linda's hair hasn't been this long for 30years. She has declined my offer to cut it.
After me bragging about the improvement in the weather, the meteorological worm has turned and since yesterday it has been raining quite heavily most of the time, and set to continue for about 10 days. There have been 'inondations' in the valley

about once every 80 years since at least the Middle Ages. The last one was in 1940 and was very destructive. We are due for another one.

The 'Saints de Glace' is a period identified since the 'Haut Moyen Âge' associated with the saints Mamet, Pancrace and Servais on the 11th, 12th and 13th of May when we are expected to have the last frosts of the spring. Absolute tosh, of course. This year the crops will be drowned not frozen.

In passing, the 2nd of May was the feast of St. Boris. Bet Grant Shapps didn't know that.

I don't think B Johnson has fully recovered from his bout of C19. He's clearly lost weight, which is perhaps no bad thing, but I'm not sure he has got a grip yet, and by all accounts this illness can leave you drained for some time. Those of you with first hand experience might like to comment.

Pork and prunes for dinner, that should keep me going.

Beware the second wave.

Cheers
Andrew

So, Little Richard died at the weekend aged 87. I really can't claim familiarity with his music except when it was covered by the Beatles or referred to by the Stones. Tutti Frutti was his first success, it was covered by Pat Boone, nauseatingly. He managed to strip out all of the raw energy and sex, leaving an anodyne rendition which passed the morality police of white American entertainment. That was in 1956 when the BBC Light Program was playing Doris Day and Frankie Laine. Live pop music on tv was Pinky and Perky, a pair of puppet pigs with electronically altered high squeaky voices, or the Billy Cotton Band with singer Alan Breeze doing covers of safe bland hits. Little Richard started the revolution.

As we are shopping much less frequently, we have to make the most of our vegetables. Cauliflower leaves go into the green soup along with the tough ends of asparagus, and the leaves of celery, cauliflower stalks get cut up and are added to the Madhur Jaffrey spicy potatoes, and potato peelings become crisps (put them in a bowl, add oil and salt, mix with your hand, lay on cooking paper on a baking sheet, stick in a hot oven for a few mins till turning golden and crispy. Linda's cheese straws are better.)

Whenever we drive down the mountain our phones ping with a message from EE welcoming us to Spain. We used to think this was a bit of a laugh, but it's no longer funny now the border is closed.

On Monday lockdown restrictions were relaxed allowing two people to get in the same car and go shopping. Some of you will be familiar with Le Pertus, a border town south of Le Boulou. It is basically a cheap shopping venue, with eat all you like buffets, street hucksters and whores. People flock there for cheap booze and cigarettes. Some people buy cheap meat and vegetables. There's loads of tourist tat, perfume and leather goods.
What I didn't know about Le Perthus is that the main road, the D900, which runs through the town to the old pre Schengen border post is French, but the pavements and the shops are Spanish. How does that work ?
Anyway, all the shops were closed during full lockdown. Some of them reopened on Monday. The place was mobbed from both countries with people desperate for their fix of cheap 'Scotch' whiskey with names you never heard of, like William Lawson, and bales of fags. The road had to be closed. There were police 'incidents'.

Facebook is a funny old thing isn't it? Since lockdown my Facebook has been full of advertisements for ladies underwear. Companies like Livy, Home and Garden Savvy (Lingeries Grandes Tailles), Wolf and Badger, Estella Lingerie. The list goes on. In the interests of academic research I've taken a look at a couple of them and I have to report that there are women out there wearing the most spectacularly uncomfortable looking underwear. I'm not complaining, it lightens my day. But what is Facebook up to? What do they think they're doing. Suppose I have a stroke, will they be held responsible? Why do they think I need all these adverts? What do they think they know about me?

Isn't Wolf and Badger a wonderful name for a company making sexy knickers?

Went to see our financial advisor today. He is one of those young Dutch men, 6ft.6in., lean and fit with long feet (think Jar Jar Binks, but rather better looking). We've filled in our first tax forms and seem to have a large tax deduction, so all is good.

Shopping in Intermarché, about 20% of shoppers not following government instructions to wear a mask, one gent holding his mask in his hand and putting it up to his mouth to speak to the cashier, the woman behind us in the queue, right up close, ignoring my suggestion she move, more concerned that someone might push in- she may have a point.

Weather still grim., Bisous all, Andrew

WOP-BOP-A-LOO-MOP, ALOP-BOM-BOM
Been practicing my tribute to Little Richard.

Well, it's been an interesting week. We've been out to dinner. Went up to
Lou Poun on Wednesday evening. They are keeping busy by constructing a garage.
This involves moving large amounts of ready mixed concrete. Andy, who seems to do
most of the heavy lifting, could hardly move for a sore back. I would offer to help, or
maybe not. It was strange being greeted by Andy and Fabien who normally hug, and
Ian who shakes my hand and kisses Linda. This time we all stood apart greeting but
not touching like traditionally awkward English as described by Kate Fox in Watching
the English. As they have been just about as isolated as we have it didn't seem to be
a worry sitting down to eat together.

The Léca Assassin (part 1).

Up the mountain there is a long established commune of hippies who call themselves
the Rainbow people. They are camped in teepees, yurts and ramshackle dwellings
constructed around various dilapidated campervans, Ford transits etc. For many
years our only awareness of the group was when we saw people hitchhiking up the
hill - we gave a few of them lifts but they were uniformly malodorous so we stopped
doing that -and in the heat of summer you could hear the ghostly sound of distant
drums.
The land is owned by a land banking consortium in Lichtenstein who have no real
interest in the land at all and have apparently given the Rainbows permission to
camp there. The hippies seem to be mostly harmless but there is occasional trouble.
They have dogs. The sheep farm is on adjacent land. The dogs are not controlled and
quite regularly kill sheep. There is suspicion that the hippies are quite partial to a bit
of lamb stew.
In recent months 20 sheep have been killed. One of the young woman from the farm
confronted the owner of one of the responsible dogs, and managed to prevail upon
him to dispatch his dog with her bolt gun. As a result, the 'Leader' of the group
turned up at the farm, threatening reprisal.

Vilalte is a large Mas with associated farm buildings renovated and converted for use
as retreat/ music summer school etc residential property. It is immediately south of
the rainbow camp. The owner, Costantino, a 78 yr old Italian former engineering
professor is currently there alone with a female assistant, whilst his wife is locked
down in England with their children. The property is a large rambling group of
buildings, vegetable gardens and a pool. Recently, Costantino noticed that a fence

had been damaged. He also noticed that his Bobcat had been moved and the engine was hot. Entering his kitchen he found a rainbow resident busy charging his mobile phone. 'I didn't think you'd mind,' he said. He also admitted responsibility for the damage and for using the Bobcat, again 'I didn't think you'd mind.' He promised to repair the damage. Dream on.

On Thursday we went for apéro at the School House to celebrate Laure's 35th birthday. Gatherings of up to 10 socially distancing people are now allowed. There were indeed 10 adults. It seems children don't count because there were 6 of them too. It was there that we learned of the stabbing......

The Léca Assassin (Part 2).

Roger, The Butcher of Arles, lives with our next door neighbour. Despite being 71 and having had heart surgery and diabetes he continues to rise at 4am to go to work, returning for lunch then back to work till 6pm, with a half day on Sunday and Monday off.
We rarely emerge from our house before 9 or 10 in the morning and had noticed that for several days Roger's car was parked outside through the day.
It turned out that Roger had been stabbed in the belly.
Well, actually, he stabbed himself. He was doing that Butcher thing where he was trimming meat by ripping towards himself. Isn't that why they always used to wear heavy leather aprons? So he stabbed himself. Blood everywhere. Sapeurs-pompiers called. Whisked him off to the Clinic du Vallespir, then on to Medipol in Perpignan for a scan. Fortunately he didn't penetrate his peritoneum but just confined himself to stabbing belly fat. So a few sutures. Michèle, who coined the phrase, the Léca Assassin, says his belly looks like a giant aubergine. Despite the pain from the extensive bruising, Roger continues to rise at 4am to go and prepare for the day, returning at 8am leaving his nephew in charge. I muttered something about 'Hari Kiri', Garlic laughed, not sure Michèle appreciated the joke.

We anticipate some improvement in the weather next week. Which will be nice.

Socially distant sounds a bit autistic don't you think?

Curry tonight

Chin chin
Andrew

P.S. Garlic is Laure's husband. Really, that's his name

Hyperbaric Chamber   24/05/20

Hi All.
Another week passes. Spring turns into summer. We've had some hot days this week.
All too late for the cherry harvest though. It has been 80% down this year. This has been attributed to the more or less continuous heavy rain for long periods in spring with no compensatory warm sunshine. Also you apparently need a freezing episode, or at the least , a winter cold snap, to initiate the cycle. How does that work? Last winter was mild. We had a bit of snow in Léca but there was none in the valley. This year there are none of the roadside cherry stalls. We bought some at Intermarché and at Co-op at double last year's price. They were pretty tasteless, not sweet and went off quickly. But tradition was preserved with a basket of the first récolte going to the Élysée Palace for the President.

Last Sunday we had the resident conspiracy theorist over for lunch. It was interesting to hear an alternative view of things. In summary: the virus thing isn't real, there are no excess deaths, there is going to be a second wave engineered by governments to control us all, ventilation kills, oxygen can be delivered through the skin using hyperbaric chambers, David Icke may have a few good ideas but is being gagged by government.....we sat outside for drinks and ate a very nice meal. I wasn't involved in cooking so nothing was burnt. When he arrived he announced that he hadn't brought wine because ours is always better (correct), but he presented us with a basket full of artichokes and asparagus from his large vegetable garden.
Growing up in the Midlands in the 50s and 60s I don't think I ever saw a globe artichoke. Actually, come to think of it, I probably never saw asparagus either. Only 50% of our household enjoy artichokes so I get to prepare and eat them. These ones were relatively small and were steamed for about 25min. The outer petals are disappointing, with very little to eat, but then you reach the inner thin pale petals which can be all pulled off together, dipped in vinaigrette, or Helmans and balsamic and eaten. No evidence of the furry choke found in the bigger ones, so the base and stalk can be eaten too. A perfect amuse bouche.

Lockdown is easing. There's a lot more traffic around. Friends in Céret say it's almost as though nothing has happened, infernal motor scooters buzzing up and down the street, lack of distancing etc..The Céret Saturday market has restarted, food only, one way traffic.
On Wednesday we went down to Arles. Where the bridge crosses the River Têch there is a picnic area under trees. Jon and Jude joined us and we had lunch with a box of rosé. The trouble with wine boxes is that you can't see how much you've had.

On Thursday, Linda visited the Beautician in Amélie with the usual remarkable results, but we then found other shops were closed. It was Ascension Day.

The beautician is having a hard time. Appointment only, mask, visor, tabard. After each client she has to do a 20min. clean of the treatment area. Clients also have to wear a mask. Until she gets to treating the moustache area.

Friday, to La Taillede for lunch with Gina and Nigel who have been staying at home from the start of lockdown. They remain very anxious, but that didn't stop Nigel from giving Linda a bear hug and kiss- her first from anyone(other than me obvs) since March 18th. La Taillede, Mas Lou Poun, Vilalte- all of these properties have been developed at great expense to provide holidays and retreats and all are suffering from a total loss of income, but they still have to pay their Tax d'Habitation and Tax Foncière, huge amounts compared to our little bills. There is apparently a set government business support grant of 1500€ per month, regardless of size of the enterprise.

As summer arrives, so do the flies. A couple of days ago I was having a mackerel for dinner. I unwrapped it and left it on the kitchen surface. Within minutes it was decorated with fly eggs. Doing the hoovering yesterday, I noticed a little cloud of the beggars dancing round in the sitting area. I invented a new sport. I took the brush head off the hoover pipe, and found that I could hoover them up from the air. Some of them accelerated away when the pipe approached but if I persevered I eventually caught the lot. Much more fun than hoovering up spiders in the bathroom. Unfortunately the flies were replaced by another team within minutes. Clearly, as a sport, fly hoovering is still in its infancy, rather like bog snorkelling , but I think I'm ready to initiate an International Federation to oversee development of the rule book, and to supervise competition. Perhaps this is something for the EPFC to manage. (some of you will be unfamiliar with the EPFC, the Emmeline Pankhurst Fan Club, a learned society of anglophone gentlemen dedicated to the memory of the sainted Emmeline, who meet at lunchtime several times a year in the Vallespir for exchange of ideas about matters of moment, and votes for women, and to eat and drink. Sadly we are not yet in a position to set the next gathering.)

Happy to report that our neighbour, Garlic, having lost his first two chickens to the fox not because the fox was smart, but because after a few beers Garlic forgot to lock the chickens in the coop, now has further developed the chicken run with a roof over one end and a further enclosure round the coop so even if Mr Fox jumps over the wall he won't be able to get at the chickens. Just so long as Garlic remembers to lock up.

After our initial enthusiasm, the walking program has faltered and we haven't been for a walk of any significance for a week.

Dominic Cummings, eh! Will he stay or will he go? I fancy he'll last another couple of days. Remember, you should only, reasonably and legally, drive 250miles to your second home, whilst falling ill with a potentially lethal illness known to cause high

fever and extreme fatigue, thus dangerously impairing your judgement and ability to drive, to deliver your small child to the care of your elderly, vulnerable parents (ed. shirly shome mishtake , it was his sister.), taking with you your already sick highly infectious wife, if there is no-one, literally No-One, family, friends, no-one who could offer assistance to you in your hour of need. Got it?
I don't think we've actually heard the truth yet.

I think that's all the news that is fit to print.
Dick Turpin used to wear a mask and look where it got him.

Duster   30/05/20

Greetings. Another weekend arrives.
Chickens don't like onion skins but love cold spaghetti and corn cobs. I know this
because Garlic has replaced the two taken by the fox with five more and they benefit
from our food waste. Garlic and family have now gone away for a week to Laure's
parents who live slightly more than the allowed 100k away leaving Michèle to guard
the chucks and water the crops. Two of the 5 chucks belong to Andy and Fabien. How
they know which eggs are theirs is an unresolved question.

We went up to Batére for a walk to the tower. There were raptors, too distant to
identify but a pair circling were huge with long primaries. I think they were griffon
vultures. A few years ago we set off to walk to the tower. Ahead of us on the crest
we saw a large group of griffons circling and perching. At the first corner we
encountered a couple gazing through binoculars back the way we had come. We
asked if they had seen the vultures behind them. They had, but they had also seen an
even bigger and closer group on the rocks across the road from the car park. There
was a dead cow below the road by the GR10 path down to Arles. The vultures were
waiting for the belly to burst.
As we walked we heard a cuckoo. I have also in recent days heard a woodpecker,
and, I think, a Golden Oriole (in Ann and Keith's garden) and seen the newly arrived
swallows and swifts. I'm no good at recognising birdsong even of the birds we have
been watching on our feeders through the spring. A man on Spring Watch said we
should learn three birdsongs a year. Bit late for me.
At Batère we saw some evidence to indicate that French restrictions are being
broken. The were vehicles from Haute Garonne (possibly ok), Essonne just south of
Paris and Karlsruhe! On the road we are seeing more Spanish cars and one Belgian.
They could all be local residents...

It has been brought to my attention by my Paris corespondent that Michel Piccoli has
died......I know, you're all devastated (that being the 'mot courant' for friends of the
departed) but you needn't be, he was 94 and had a 70 year career in film. He's one of
those actors who seems to be in every French film that doesn't have J P Belmondo
and, despite his receding hairline and unremarkable looks he apparently, according
to my source (DF), kissed all the most beautiful women in the industry. (I see that in
1945 he was rather handsome.) He was married three times, once to Juliette Gréco,
and had three children, two of whom have silly names. I first saw him in Belle de Jour
at the Jacey on Princes Street in Edinburgh in 1967. Some of you will be familiar with
the Jacey Cinema Chain. It specialised in 'Art House Movies', mostly French, Italian
and Swedish and guaranteed that you would see more of the leading lady's skin than
was allowed by Hollywood, at a time when married couples slept in twin beds and

kept one foot on the floor. The Jacey closed in 1973, became a Gap store and is now a listed building. When I was a Medical Student some of us would go occasionally on wet Wednesday afternoons. Pete Burns, a physically unattractive chap with thick lensed black framed specs, crooked teeth and a monster overbite, but who, nevertheless managed to charm a series of beautiful young women in to his bed, was too mean to pay his 1s3p entrance and would wait till we were in then knock on the fire escape door for one of us to let him in. Of course the management soon got wise and put an alarm on the door. Pete's medical career was ended after one year probably because he did absolutely no studying and he left Edinburgh to study pharmacy elsewhere. I'm sure he did very well.

I think I mentioned that our Contrôle Technique was overdue. We mentioned this to Tony & Lucy who realised that theirs was also out of date. They are stuck in London and their Duster is garaged at Mas Cazenove, just up the road from us beyond the farm. We offered to deal with this. We walked up to Mas Caz. to fetch the car. The garage is the grange at the back of the house. Entering the grange we found that the Duster, which hasn't moved since January, and has been sharing space with wildlife including recently arrived and nesting swallows, was covered with dust (appropriately), leaves, droppings etc. The engine started first time. To exit the garage you have to drive up a steep narrow incline with a wall of rock to your right and a sheer drop to your left. The pathway is unmade, with grass and weeds (ed. Shouldn't that be 'wild flowers?) over a foot high. I proceeded with caution. As I began to increase the revs to try to mount the incline the car started to skid sideways towards the cliff edge. Then I stalled. I rolled back. I tried again five times. The result was the same each time. I decided that I wasn't prepared to risk life and limb, put the car back and we set off to walk home again.

At the farm we met Siska and explained our problem. She told her father and he offered to help. Antoine is our Mayor, a bear of a man with massive hands and forearms. I don't understand how he plays the mandolin but that's another story. Antoine returned with us to the Duster, got in, started the engine, and took off... The car erupted out or the garage and disappeared over the hill to the gate, only slightly bouncing off the rock wall with me trailing behind shouting to Linda, 'Tell him I hate him!' We took the Duster down to the CT

testing station in Amélie. It is a one man band. The man in question is the definition of lugubrious, tall, stooped with black receding slightly too long hair, calling to mind Uncle Fester in The Munsters. The Duster got a clean bill of health and Uncle Fester smiled.

On Thursday we drove to Céret for lunch with friends. At the hairpin bend at the top of Corsavy we met a Spanish car reversing round the bend. As I passed I shouted some ritual abuse, naturally. Pulling round the corner I was confronted by a Sappeur Pompiers Ambulance blocking the street, lights flashing. I had to reverse and follow the Spaniard on the bypass and down the hill. Embarrassing.

We later learned that André Blanch, 62, President of the Chasse de Corsavy, had died. I think Michèle told me if I understood correctly that he had cancer and was awaiting treatment, presumably delayed by C19. He once gave me his share of the days sanglier meat.

Summer is definitely on the way. I've made my first gazpacho of the year and Keith's pool is warm enough for Linda to swim. Bliss.

So when do you all think you'll be back in PO? Missing you all.

Andrew

It'a Sunday again.

It's been raining for much of the last week. Sometimes the rain has been heavy. Sometimes the rain has been very heavy. Sometimes the rain has been torrential. In between the rain Linda managed to go to the coiffeuse in Le Boulou. She made an appointment on line which only allowed her to book a cut and blow dry. Highlights are not available on line. I never knew how grey her hair had become.

With the rain the temperature has dropped so we are not swimming in our friends' pool.

We managed a socially distant walk round the lake at St. Jean Pla de Corts. There are notices up allowing walking, running and cycling, anything dynamic, but no sitting, picnicking or swimming. You can walk your dog, though not on the grass. There were a couple of exercise classes for old people going on. One class seemed to be practicing turning their heads, and the other were doing slight bending from the waist. Looked a bit energetic for me.

On Wednesday we had Jon and Jude up for lunch. They arrived in an electric storm. Jon, gent that he is, dropped Jude at the door then went to park the car. As he arrived at our door a lightning bolt struck the electricity pylon two meters away followed instantly by a tremendous crash of thunder. The house shook. The circuit breaker blew, the lights went off. Jon was remarkable calm about this near death event.

We pushed the circuit breaker back in and everything was working except the broadband which always goes off in electric storms. It resumed later when the storm

had past. Michèle next door had more trouble. She lost her router, parabole, tv decoder and telephone. It's a mystery why she had so much damage and we had nothing. Could it be because our system isn't earthed? Does the surge perceive our system as a blind offshoot of

Michèle's whilst hers gives it a route to earth?
After a week of rain and the prospect of another wet week to come, we are off to an Airb&b in the Camargue on Tuesday for 5 nights. It may still be raining there but it should be a bit warmer and will surely be below the clouds. Unlike Léca:

Restaurants and bars have started to open again. In Céret the other day we saw Marie, the front of house at Le France, in mask and gloves with cloth and spray, cleaning tables and chairs between customers.
Jon tells us that the Bar Pablo has reopened with a completely new équipe.

As John Steinbeck said, 'Oh, strawberries don't taste as they used to and the thighs of women have lost their clutch'. Quite what relevance that has to anything I'm not sure but if I ever write a novel it's the quote I shall have at the start. Classy novelists always have mysterious quotes at the beginning. I've just read De Bernières' So Much Life Left To Live. He does it. Excellent book by the way. He writes very well.
Any recommendations for my next read? I'm now reading Ian McEwan's The Innocent which has turned a bit grizzly.

Who's writing a lockdown novel?

À bientôt
Andrew

Léca Diaries, Camargue Édition

The incessant rain and cold in Léca drove us to find something a little more congenial. We identified an Airb&b in an old farm complex between Saint Gilles and Saintes Maries de la Mare in the Camargue east of Montpellier and west of Arles. We arrived on Tuesday afternoon in warm sunshine. An elderly gentleman in a broad brimmed hat was sitting outside the main house. He hauled himself to his feet and ambled over accompanied by a large and equally slow long haired alsacien dog. We had already identified that the ivy covered building attached to the end of the main house was indeed the Pigeonier which we had booked. He invited us to make ourselves at home pending the arrival of his wife who had gone to Nîmes.

The appartement consisted of an open plan ground floor with kitchen and living room, a narrow steep wooden Pigeonier stair with narrow treads and no handrails leading to the first floor, two bedrooms, bathroom (with Linda's pet hate, the plastic shower curtain), loo.

Shortly after we had installed ourselves, a small grey Mercedes pulled up across the yard and a figure emerged. It was female, small and slim, dressed in a tan coloured shirt dress, with a hemline at mid thigh. She collected several bags. They were those shiny stiff paper bags with logos and rope handles, the sort of bags that shops give you to take away the very expensive underwear, perfume or shoes w hich madam has spent a fortune on. Carrying the bags in one hand she set off towards us, her free hand flailing sideways to maintain balance. She was walking on very high heel platform rope espadrilles, like a mannequin on the catwalk, one foot in front of the other, as though on a tightrope, hips swivelling, all lipstick and mascara. The dress was unbuttoned to her diaphragm, revealing a brown breast which was desperately struggling to escape. This was Nicole, the owner. She had reached her three score years and ten with clearly no intention of subsiding into graceful old age just yet. She was charming and helpful. She changed the livebox which we could not get to work because the previous tenants, not for the first time she said, had taken it upon themselves to change the wifi code! She informed us that she had a femme de menage who kept the place clean, so we didn't like to point out to her the remains of a nest around a light fitting and the bird droppings on the walls. You can't get the staff these days.

There are three male peacocks in the grounds, which frequently display their tail feathers. I'm a bit mystified by this, the mating season is January, and there are no females to impress. They must be amongst the noisiest birds. They start calling at about 04.00 and continue through the day till dusk when they fly up into a tree for the night.

The Camargue is delightful. It's very flat, a refreshing contrast to the Vallespir. There is lots of water. The lower end of the Rhône passes through to the sea. There are canals, étang, rice paddies, marais, beaches, ancient churches, delightful towns. The famous white horses are available to ride, but I decided that asking one to carry me would qualify as 'cruel and unusual punishment'. There are bird reserves, the stars of which are herons and egrets with fledglings, flamingos, glossy ibis, and bee eaters. This morning, and all day, it has been blowing a gale. We went to Saintes Marie de la Mer, named after not one, not two, but three saints called Mary who all allegedly pitched up here after the crucifixion though I think the provenance is very questionable. We walked along the front in the very strong wind, doing silent movie impressions. I had some oysters, then we had a fishy lunch in a delightful restaurant. Mask on till you reach your table, and on again to go to the loo. Waitress with expensive looking mask positioned below her nose, sanitising tables and chairs between customers.

Tomorrow we are going to Aiguës Mortes so hope it doesn't rain too much, then back to Léca on Sunday. It's been hot and sunny in Corsavy today, more rain forecast for all next week.

The bit covered in ivy is where we're staying.

Your 4am alarm call.

Stay vigilant. Eat cake. Drink wine.

Andrew

Greetings all.

We returned from La Camargue on Sunday 14th. Unfortunately we got our timing wrong and drove through Fitou at lunchtime when the wine outlets were closed. Our trip to Aigues Mortes the previous day was abortive. Saturday lunchtime is not a good time to visit a major tourist attraction just after release of lockdown. The carparks were full. We eventually found a space in an overflow carpark some distance from the entrance to the mediaeval town. As we walked away from the car the heavens opened. We scurried back to the car and quickly came to the conclusion that this was not a good idea.

We set off to Saintes Maries. There is an alternative route marked Bac Sauvage so we took it. We drove through delightful Carmaguaise countryside until we reached the river. The Petit Rhône blocked our way. There was a chain ferry. Which was free. But this was France, and it was lunchtime. The ferry was closed for lunch. There was a shack by the road side which advertised itself as a restaurant. It looked rather shabby so we didn't go in but returned to the main road and went to Saintes Marie's where we found a decent place to eat. I looked up the restaurant by the ferry later. It had excellent reviews.

As we left the motorway at Le Boulou the blue skies and sunshine gave way to cloud and falling temperatures. By the time we arrived home we were in the clouds.

The next three days we spent shopping, cooking, and staring out of the window at the rain. It was cold, but you can't seriously light a fire in the south of France in June. Do you remember those days when you couldn't hardly go out except to shop or to get a prescription, when there was no spaghetti to be had, you tried to limit your use of toilet paper, you passed the time making useless masks out of old t-shirts, or the wife's spent thongs, and when you went out you took an 'attestation'?

Well it's all different now. At least in France. Not like New Zealand though (smug b*****ds). Is the warm feeling I get on hearing that Germany's R number is now nearly 3 called schadenfreude?

Restaurants are open. On Thursday we went to La Dulcine at Reynes for lunch which was delightful. On Saturday we went to Chez Françoise in Corsavy for lunch. Terrific. On Sunday we were invited to our friends Francette and Alfred in Amélie for lunch. They are somewhat older than us and of a rather conservative mind. The walls are decorated with pictures of Napoleon, as were the coffee cups. They don't have children, they have dogs. When we first met them many years ago, after we had been spending summers in Léca for 10 or 15 years and they had decided to acknowledge us, they used to have a dog called Tendresse, but when she was bad Francette called her Ségolène, which she regarded as a gross insult, referencing as it did the Socialist politician, and then mistress of the future President François Holland, Ségolène Royal. We daren't ask them what they think of Donnie 'Bonespurs' Trump.

Despite our very obvious political differences, they are excellent, if sometimes unusual hosts. Being dog lovers, they don't really understand my aversion to having a dog suddenly emerging from under the table to thrust its snout into my genital area whilst I'm poised with a forkful of blanquette half way to my mouth.

Have you ever had lamprey? No, well nor had we. Then a couple of years ago they invited us for lunch and gave us lamprey. As Wikipedia puts it, Lamprey are an ancient extant lineage of jawless fish. They are blood sucking parasites. And they are a bordelaise delicacy. King Henry 1st, fourth son of William the Conqueror, and therefore Norman French though born in Selby, North Yorkshire, is said to have died of a surfeit of lampreys. It'll never happen to me. The dish presented to us had a rather slimy texture and earthy taste. But it was an unforgettable experience. Not to be repeated.

It's stopped raining for a few days, the sun is shining and it's warming up. Went to Keith's pool this morning for a swim. The water was 26C. Too cold for Mrs Evans but I managed a few lengths just to show I'm well 'ard.

Our broadband is once again awful. I phoned Orange English Speaking 'helpline'. I got the usual rude Russian female. Me 'Please stop shouting at me.' Her 'I'M NOT SHOUTING'. Same speil we always get about upgrading the equipment. Nothing she can do. I just tried to download a photo to attach to this email but it wouldn't work, so god knows if the email will send.

Happy days Andrew

How do you like your toast?   27/06/20

Hi there everyone.

I'm confused. How many people can I meet. Inside or out, relatives or friends, Bournemouth beach or Durdle Door, how far can I travel, can I cross the border, how long must I quarantine, which statues can I safely admire, one meter or two, mask or no mask, can I demonstrate, and, if so, what for, where, when? Whatever happened to the Gillets Jaunes??

Rather depressed to hear that Marine Le Pen's ex, Louis Aliot, is probably going to become Maire of Perpignan. The large North African community must be over the moon.

A week ago, the computer in our car informed us, in Spanish, that the car needed a service. Now, as you know, we live 1000m up a mountain, and some of the road surfaces are a bit rough. Whenever we descend the mountain we spend most of the time breaking. I have been told that the alternative is to drive in low gear but I can't imagine that that does the engine or the clutch any good. I once asked Gilles, the garagiste, why he seemed to need to change our tyres rather more frequently than I was accustomed to. "What do you think?" He replied, "You don't live in Paris." So we were aware that our front tyres were, how to say, …bald. We also started to hear that ominous grating noise which we have learned means that the brake pads are disintegrating. We told Gregoire, who has taken over from his uncle Gilles, and he declared it an emergency, he gave us an appointment two days later.

The service was done yesterday. It was too late. The front brake pads had completely gone and the discs were foutou. So new discs, pads and tyres. €€€.

Gilles is charming, always a jolly smile, thin and bald, he rides a hot motorbike and plays guitar in a jazz/rock band with our insurance agent Frank. Gilles' wife is the rather dour, chain-smoking, horse riding Flo who used to work in the office. A couple of years ago they handed over the running of the garage to nephew Gregoire. He came from Paris where he worked in HR in some huge business in La Défence. As far as we can make out he had no previous background in car mechanics, but he seems to be learning fast and has an enthusiastic, cheerful, 'can do' attitude. They get things done quickly.

Before the car was returned to me it was sanitised.

How do you like your toast? I ask because this is a major issue between me and the current Mrs. Evans. I like it singed, golden brown, even a little black at the edges, and crispy so that when you spread the butter you can hear the knife scraping the surface. Mrs. E, by contrast, likes hers warmed and dried in the toaster but with no discernible colour change. How is that toast? It's just warmed bread, dry on the surface and limp inside. The result is Toaster Wars. I turn the dial up, she turns it

down. If the toast comes out brown or black she turns up her nose saying, "How can you EAT that?" Well, frankly, if there's too much pure charcoal on the surface it just needs a bit if a scrape then lots of butter and jam (other spreads are available, though how anyone can eat marmalade I'll never understand, and as for marmite, well I'll say nothing.) When I was growing up, you couldn't waste toast just because it was singed unless it came out from under the grill (no such thing as a toaster) actually in flames. No smoke alarms back then.
And don't get me started on crumpets.

I last had an exhibition in Céret in Salle Manolo in August 2018. Since then I have been finding it difficult to create paintings which I am happy to show. I was offered the same slot this summer. After long discussions with my management team (Linda), I have decided that I don't have enough for a show and am not in a creative state of mind, so I have cancelled. The immediate result of this is that we have booked another little trip. We are off to the Ardèche next Tuesday for a week. We have a place to stay in Vallon Pont d'Arc and will be exploring the Gorges of the Tarn. Any recommendations?

Summer has arrived.

As far as I can make out, the safest way to engage socially is as follows: meet outside only with the person with whom you share a bed, do not shake hands, no hugging or kissing (definitely NO TONGUES), wear a mask, wash your hands every two minutes whilst singing Happy Birthday twice or reciting the opening credits from Startreck as far as the split infinitive. Sit two meters apart, back to back and converse. DO NOT SHOUT. Stop fiddling with your mask, it doesn't work if pulled down on to your chin. If you can't hear each other, use a mobile phone. You will then of course have to wear gloves and sanitize the keyboard with a babywipe. When you've done all that, have several large gin'n'tonics and jump in a hot tub. Together. Further details should not be necessary.

I hope that's helpful.
Must go now, the men in white coats have arrived.

Cheers

Andrew

Greetings Francophiles. (Autocorrect was a bit busy there but I got the better of it.)

A week ago we set off from the meteorologically challenged Vallespir to use up some Home Exchange points of which we have several million, to spend a week in the Ardèche. The property we have is a two bedroom house in a development which is new but meant to look 'traditional' with irregular limestone facing. There is a dark wood spiral staircase poorly lit, with the only loo downstairs. Not ideal at my age. There is a small secluded garden with mature trees including mulberry and eucalyptus, and three hammocks. I like a hammock. I find them comfortable and enjoy the gentle too and fro. But they are a bitch to get out of. First time I had to roll out onto my knees and haul myself up using the tree. Second time my lovely assistant came and gave me her hand and used her weight leaning back to get me out and upright. So undignified.

On our first morning, as we were sitting down to lunch at 13.00 the man next door started with his electric sander, 3m away, through a thick laurel hedge. I waited for a pause in the noise and called to him that we were sitting down to lunch outside. He responded that in France one could make a noise between 8am and 6pm and carried on. But only for a minute to prove his point.

The Pont d'Arc is astounding. The Ardèche river, over millennia has carved a sinuous gorge through the limestone. The stone bridge was formed when a meander broke through.

"So, we're not doing the fish today, we're doing the lavender and the snails." Thus I was greeted on the morning of Friday 3rd by my resident tour guide. Wha....?
We drove along the spectacular Gorge de l'Ardèche. There are frequent 'belvederes'. These are viewing points where you are invited to walk up to the edge of a cliff, or indeed out beyond, protected from plunging to certain death by a guard rail which comes up only to where my waist used to be. I'm no longer clear about where my centre of gravity resides. I have difficulty controlling my sphincters. My tour guide dances around like a careless fairy.

Then to Escargot des Restang where we met Cyrille, a snail farmer. He gave us a tour of his enterprise. I honestly can't remember most of the numbers but here's what I've got. There are basically three types of snails which are cultivated for consumption, grey snails (small & large, same sp.) grown in France, Borgougne grown in eastern France and through to Eastern Europe and Turq grown in Italy and the levant. They are all in the Genus Helix, true snails. There is a monster grown in the Far East which is often served as snails, but look for the ingredients, if it doesn't list Helix it ain't snail.

Snails can travel at up to 4m per hour. After hermaphrodite reproduction involving erotic darts (honest!), eggs are laid which Cyrille brings on in his shed. When they are ready he puts them in his field which has rows of wooden 'tents', and lots of snail food plants. They are prevented from escaping by electrified strips around the field. Predators, which include sanglier, rats, mice, snakes are inhibited from entering by electric wires, and predator passerine birds are minimised by the fortunate presence of Bonelli's Eagles.

There is no charge for the tour but understandably Cyrille invites you to buy his snail based products at the end. Hmmm, Christmas presents.

More later. Andrew

We were in the southern Ardèche which is essentially a huge slab of limestone with the odd extinct volcano. Over the millennia rivers have carved huge meandering gorges and there are lots of Grottes with stalagmites and stalactites. Stalactites are the ones that come down from the roof and hang on tight.

We visited several small towns and villages. We went to Ruoms for the Night Market (4pm-midnight), there was a downpour just before we arrived at 5pm and all the stall holders had given up, packed up and gone. There are so few people around I guess they are dispirited. We went into the town. It's not an attractive place, uninteresting buildings, tourist tat shops and uninviting bars. We had a drink in converted petrol station and left.

Most of the old buildings are constructed, unsurprisingly, with limestone which is to be found everywhere, often in the form of large brick shaped slabs. There was little or no sophistication or elegance in the buildings. By contrast, if you are ever in Mexico, check out the Yucatan Mayan architectural legacy, monumental, highly decorative and also limestone.

To Vallon for the Friday market, which was enormous. Quite a lot of masks being worn but social distancing gone as people jostle in the crowded lanes, bisous returning. The big church is Protestant.

We went through St. Michel, St. Juste and St. Marcel none of which had anything of interest. What do we know about Saint Marcel? I want him to be patron saint of hairdressers.

Labeaume, a little village on the river Beaume, is delightful but probably absolutely rammed in high season. From there we went to Vogüé. Obviously I want to be able to boast that we were 'in vogue' but disappointingly it's pronounced 'Vo-joo-eh'. This is also a spectacular village on the Ardèche river. We had lunch at l'Esparet at a pavement table which was fine because the traffic flow was very light.

We visited the Grotte de la Madeleine. Those of you with dogs may wish to skip this paragraph. We booked on line, because you have to. Then we were instructed to print off our passes. As if you all bring your airprinter on holiday! On arrival the guidance was confusing with coloured arrows on the floor which clarified nothing. We eventually found the ticket office run by a Slovak lady, obtained our tickets and English language audio guide and arrived at the entrance. Other visitors gathered including lots of children. Then a couple with three children and a dog. And what a dog. A large heavy young Alsatian. The woman was in charge of the dog. Except she wasn't. The dog was far stronger than her, and he was in charge. I couldn't believe it. They were bringing the dog into the cave system. Our guide appeared and started to talk. She was wearing a mask, we all were, except the highly infectious small children. And the dog. The guide was almost impossible to hear, muffled by her mask. The audio guide seemed to have a completely different text. There were 200 wet slippery steps down into the system. At the first steep section the dog balked and we were all held up whilst it's owners cajoled and carried it down. To be fair, the dog actually behaved, though how much it learned about spéléologie I don't know. If you're thinking of going, don't bother. It's a pretty poor show. Les Grandes Canallettes is far superior.

At this point I was going to bang on about lavender, but we just got back to Léca, I'm knackered and I'm going to bed.

Pip pip

Andrew

Good morning campers.

Refreshed by a night's sleep, drinking tea in the morning sunshine and admiring all the spiders' webs which have appeared in our absence.

So, to the Musée de Lavendre which is actually a lavender farm with a visitor center including a large bar, beer on tap, light snacks, and a shop where you can purchase all things lavender. It was hot so I had un demi. The parking was not full so I was enraged to watch as both wheelchair spaces nearest to the entrance were taken by two manifestly fit couples, one with Paris plates. I know, I know, you can't always see the handicap. They probably had agoraphobia or piles, all sorts of possibilities come to mind. All I can say is they showed no signs of mobility issues. I, being British, muttered into my beer.

The tour started with the road train driven by the raven haired Natalie. She informed us that she was the wife of the great grandson of the berger who had the land as uncultivated garrigue on which he kept sheep and goats. The fields are now row upon row of lavender plants of varying maturity, in full bloom, an assault on the eyes and the nose. The original animal building was now the café bar. They grow three varieties of lavender, the 'fine' which gives small quantities of high grade oil for the perfume industry, an intermediate one and a third, which is a natural hybrid, which produces large quantities of lower grade oil for your furniture polish.

Arriving at the main buildings we saw a film then had a one hour lecture from Natalie on how the business had developed and how the oil was extracted. It could have been half as long and twice as interesting, but I managed to get some of it. The oil is distilled using an alembic originally devised by mediaeval alchemists, a large copper still of simple design. At the end of the tour we saw a still in action, water and oil, and a certain amount of plant debris trickled into a glass bottle, the oil separated and rose to the top, with a layer of debris separating it trom the flower scented water. Natalie explained that this was 'physics'. The oil was decanted from the top.

If you cut plants back to the woody stems they die. To grow a new plant, take a cutting in autumn, including wooden stem, strip down to white wood for a couple of cm. on one side, leave in water to encourage root growth, then bury it 9 tenths in poor soil with stones to help drainage. Water once. Then leave entirely alone, only watering lightly if there is a canicule. Cut back the new growth in autumn even if it doesn't flower.

Essential oils. What's that about? What's essential about them? If they're essential, how come I've survived so long (too long some may say) without them?

Uzès, which is in Gard, is delightful. There is a small old town centred round the Duke's Palace. Robin Yapp has a place here. He was a dentist who's hobby was sourcing good wine from small growers. Very sensibly he converted his hobby into his job and established Yapp Wines (now Yapp Brothers) in Mere, Wiltshire. Here is Robin's front door:

Ten meters away across the street is the Caviste, Trésors des Vignes. We went in and introduced ourselves as friends of M. Yapp- well, we've met him on two occasions, spending several days together in Cornwall- and they greeted us with enthusiasm. We bought some of Robin's favourites and Matthieu trollied it to the car park.

This time, on our return journey we got the timing right and arrived in Fitou when the cave was open. It's under new management. Turns out the new young boss used to date Arnaud's sister. Arnaud works for the Corsavy commune, keeps the roads clear, strims the verges, general maintenance. Four terrific reds tasted, case of each bought. Set up for the summer. As a cadeau they gave us a bottle of young red from a small producer locally which they said we should keep for 3-4 years. That'll be tricky. Léca is unchanged. Going for a swim later.
Unbelievably, David Cameron appeared in my dreams last night.

Hope your summer is going well.
Andrew

Greetings Gardeners

I did try to get Monty Donn to edit this edition but he cried off muttering, before he put the phone down, something about 'reputation' and 'professional integrity'. So I approached Alan Titchmarsh. He said the project was 'bonnie' and tried to sell me a funeral plan. So I'll just have to do my best without them.

I do not come from gardening stock. My father's maternal grandfather was a farm labourer in Dorset. My Nan grew black currants in her black yard in Dudley. My parents showed no real gardening skills. Dad grew runner beans several years and there was some rhubarb at the bottom of the garden. The important thing was to keep the front privet hedge and front lawn immaculate. The back garden was a playground for us five kids.

Mrs Evans on the other hand has gardening in her blood. She inherited three things from her mother, nursing, cooking and gardening. I have no idea how they compared as nurses but I would venture to say that whilst Linda was and is the better cook her mother, Freda, won the prize for gardening. Freda was an outstanding basic English cook. Her roast Sunday lunch was a dream come true and her steak and kidney pie was unsurpassable. But it didn't work so well when she moved out of her comfort zone. Her spaghetti 'bolognaise' was.... memorable.

The garden was glorious. It helped that she lived in a cottage in rural Dorset with rich black soil and a stream at the end of the garden. She took cuttings, dunked them in a little pot of rooting powder, planted them and they grew. She grew broad beans. I love broad beans. Why d'you think I married her daughter?

In Léca we do not have a garden as such. We have a balcony and below it a small paved terrace with a low wall separating it from the jungle. We can grow things in pots and growbags. As we have spent more time here we have tried various things. We've managed potatoes in pots, and French beans. We grew a very expensive tomato one year. Just the one. Thyme, tarragon, chives and mint do well. We have struggled with parsley. The problem is that most summers it is hot and dry with little rain and there's no shade. It's difficult to keep up with the watering.

This year Linda decided to try to grow more stuff. It started with some sprouting potatoes which were cut up and planted in pots. Despite the mild, very wet winter and spring, they grew. They didn't flower but did produce an small crop of little spuds in late spring.

In the meantime came Covid 19 and lockdown. Shops and garden centres were shut. Seeds were available at Intermarché, so plastic trays of terreau were planted with lettuce, tomato, beans, courgettes, parsley and coriander. Up in the mountains it can get cold at night so we watched the temperature and brought our little children in if frost was forecast. March turned into April and seedlings emerged, it was as exciting as watching paint dry but not as fast. Soon we had loads of little tomato, lettuce, bean plants. Everything germinated. But it rained. And it rained. Friends with a house up the hill which they have lived in for 40 years had a flood in their living room. This has never happened before.

This weather is perfect for fungi. Trouble is it's not just the girolles which are thriving, it's all the plant pathogens too. The lettuce grew well but some of the leaves turned black. The French beans grew and flowered, and beans grew, but then the plants stopped flowering so were left with just the early crop.

The courgettes emerged and flowered but the new courgettes are dying and the leaves are yellow. We got one little one and ate it for dinner yesterday:

Keith's rose which we have been nurturing, has mildew, black fly and black spot. It's leaves keep dropping. Linda has transferred it to intensive care. New pot, new terreau, rose feed and sulphur. (Keith, you might want to prepare for the worst.) We went to the garden centre today and asked their advice. We came home with a packet of sulphur powder which is supposed to fix the mould. Fingers crossed. Linda scattered carrot seeds in a large pit of terreau. It now looks like a carrot lawn. We've had coriander and parsley but they are beginning to turn yellow. Worst of all are the tomato plants which stopped growing , leaves curled up and turned brown, plants died. I've put sulphur on the remainder to see if that revives them. I'm not hopeful.

In other news.

Walked to the tower at Batère the other day. On the way back we met a young man who seemed in need of dental attention judging by the black on his teeth. He was dressed just in shorts and boots, and was pushing a pram which appeared to contain all his worldly goods, which included a cat in a travel basket, and a long green noodle (maybe he likes the water but can't swim.). We hailed him in French. He responded with, "Spik eenglish?" "Yes," we replied,"where are you going?" "Bosnia," he replied and off he went.

And remember, if you do feel yourself drawn to the greenhouse, take a large glass of chilled rosé and all will be well.

Cheers,

Andrew

Entomology

Entomology   18/07/20

Greetings.

The weather has improved. We haven't had a torrential downpour for a week or so. Down on the plain it is becoming positively hot during the day, and even Léca can be hot though clouds tend to gather over the peaks in the afternoon. There has been a comet visible in the northern sky throughout the month. Unfortunately, because of mountains and clouds we have not seen it. In truth the main reason we haven't seen it is because it is best seen between 0400 and 0430.

It is fly season. Fortunately, because we are 1000m up the mountain, we aren't troubled by mosquitoes, unlike the residents of Céret.
House flies emerged some weeks ago. Whenever I lie on the couch flies think any exposed skin is somewhere to land and explore. They mill around in the kitchen landing on any exposed food to feast and lay eggs.
There are about 100,000 known species of flies. They have a single pair of membranous wings, the hind wings being reduced to minute pin shaped 'balancers'. There are many different houseflies and I can't identify which particular one we have. Fly swat, sticky strip, fly spray, nothing makes much difference.
In the last week we have also started to see larger flies, black, pale striped thorax, yellow pattern on the abdomen, large red-brown eyes. I think these are blowflies, specifically flesh flies.
When we go swimming in Keith's pool, we are plagued when we emerge by clouds of flies. They include horse flies with startling big green eyes. It's the females which use their blade like mouth parts to pierce my skin and suck blood. The males are nectar feeders. Yesterday I was stung by a smaller grey one, possibly a Cleg fly. They apparently have hairy eyes- I've had mornings like that- but as I smacked it I wasn't able to confirm the state of its eyes.
What an awful thing it must be to be a horse at this time of year. There are several horses in fields in Corsavy. Their heads are covered in flies which seek out eyes ears and nostrils. The solution is to dress the horse in a sort of burka with fine mesh to allow the animal to see. I rather suspect that the flies find their way inside anyway which must be very annoying for the poor beast.

News in brief:
Jon Everitt suffered a sheared saddle bolt (makes my eyes water just thinking about it) and sustained extensive abrasions to calf, knee, thigh and elbow. As you may

recall, Jon had a full head of curly blond locks before he came to our house recently and we arranged for him to be struck by lightning, rendering him bald, but I don't think this bicycle incident is related.

Chris and Alison are taking the Channel Tunnel on Monday and Mr and Mrs Profitpie are taking a ferry to Roscoff on 16 Aug. so a meeting of the EPFC will be arranged. Is anyone else planning to come south?

In France we must wear masks in enclosed public spaces.

The summer holidays have started and the motorway traffic is huge, beaches are open, in many ways life is returning to normal. We can go to restaurants and sit outside in Pl. Picasso having a coffee.

The only shopping shortage we have experienced is cava which caused Mrs Evans some distress. This week we were able to rectify this by Going To Spain. The border is open. Masks must be worn in public. It's not going well. Barcelona has just reentered lockdown. Nevertheless we took the very busy motorway across the border, off at junction 2 and to Capmany, and the Oliveda Cave for 6 cases of cava which should keep her happy for several weeks, and a bottle of Bridge gin to sedate my little sister when she visits later in the year.

In Mongolia a teenager has died of plague after eating a marmot. There are supposed to be marmot on the high slopes round Batère. Never seen one.

Where's Berlusconi when you need a bit of distraction?

A vaccine is coming.

Two other signs of return to normality:

1. In Corsavy the morning council of the elders, led by Janneau Boher, have reconvened for morning coffee on the small terrace at Chéz Françoise at 10.30 every morning. The one time I ventured to join them several years ago I was quizzed sternly about brexit.

2. Driving into Spain, the whores are back on the job (ed. Is that what you actually meant to say?) sporting some remarkable cut away garments. Do you think they realise how the style draws attention to their ladyparts?

Also for information, there are a whole new set of super-dooper speed cameras in 66 details available on PO Life. They seem to de replacements for the cameras burnt out by the Gilets Jaunes.

Beware the second wave.
Papillon was more interested in the seventh wave.

A

Remember; The Virus Always Waves Twice. What a great movie that's going to be.

Let me introduce you to Dr. Carrie Madej MD. She, I regret to say, is medically qualified from Mercer University, Georgia, USA. She also has a qualification in Osteopthy, and describes herself as a specialist in internal medicine which is American for Adult Physician. She is an anti-vaxer. And she is either very ignorant about science or just a liar. I thought Wakefield was bad but this person is frightening, using her medical authority to dispense fear, misinformation, distortion and rubbish science. You can see her on YouTube peddling her lies if you have 20 minutes of your life to waste.

Amongst other claims, she states that vaccines such as MMR are routinely contaminated with mycoplasma, your smart phone monitors how often you have sex! (ed. That could be useful, how can I find that function?) ,vaccines introduce DNA modification, cancer cells, toxins, god knows what into your body, the vaccine technology is about mind control. She also lies extensively about vaccine trials, claiming inter alia that no proper trials have been done, and that just because the vaccine has generated antibody doesn't mean you are protected and there is no research to check. She gets weepy and emotional at the end.

By contrast, Prof. Andrew Pollard of Oxford University, whom I have heard speak on a number of occasions at medical meetings, is a first rate medical scientist and the one I will trust.

It's beginning to look as though old people may need serial boosters in order to achieve an adequate response.

Moving on.

A new covid problem has been brought to my attention. It's the problem of going to the coiffeuse. I understand that in the past, the question to the customer, "How has your week been?" Would result in a ten minute stream of inconsequential blather about what she had been up to, whilst the child slave washed her hair. Any awkward pause would be met with the follow up, "Any plans for the week end? Are you going away this summer? Where's your next big holiday?"

Now, it goes thus:

Hairdresser: (adjusting visor) Keep your mask on dear. Have a squirt of sanitizer. Have you had a busy week?

Customer: Mff flubble smunngh.

H: What was that dear?

C: I SAID NO, BEEN AT HOME
H: Don't shout dear. Any plans for the weekend?
C: No.
H: Are you going away this summer?
C: No. (Thinks "Just driving to Barnard f*****g Castle to test my eyesight".)
H: Any big holidays planned?
C: No. ....can I have highlights?
H: Sorry. You need to book them on line.
C: silence. Starts reading a 13 year old copy of Woman's Weekly.

(Ah, the Woman's Weekly. Brings to mind the supreme, late, lamented Victoria Wood's version of the Ella Fitzgerald song, 'Lets do it', which she called 'The Ballad of Barry and Freda', with the immortal line 'Beat me on the bottom with the Woman's Weekly'. This can also be found on YouTube and is much more worth your time than Dr Madej.)

My wife had a hairdresser once who had a little car which he called Fanny. He explained that he called it this because it was the only fanny he was ever likely to get into.
In my childhood I had two Great Aunt Fannys, my brother reminds me. I only have one memory of my father's Aunt Fanny when we visited her in a care home in Battle. She died shortly afterwards and my father purchased a plot in the churchyard for her internment which is the property of his heirs in perpetuity, so, if I want to I can be buried there when my time comes. But as I am one of five I fear the plot could become rather full.
My mother's Aunt Fanny, her mother's sister, was a dotty old soul, never married, very lively, as skinny as Granny was fat, lived in an old people's home in Dudley or thereabouts. Being physically fit she acted as an unpaid assistant. It kept her occupied. Her long hair was worn up, held in place with a load of hairgrips. She clutched a handkerchief in one hand, constantly wiping her nose, dabbing her mouth, chin, cheeks, hair, pausing frequently to smother small children like us with unwelcome wet kisses.

Before I started cutting my own hair with clippers I used to go to the barber in Amélie les Bains. He is a cool laconic guy with a teddy boy haircut modelled, no doubt, on a young Johnny Hallyday. His wife is from Côte d'Ivoire. They have a lovely daughter. I went one day and he was doing an American 'flat top' crew cut, a painstaking process to get the cut even. I sat down and looked through the newspaper lying on the bench. Eventually it was done to everyone's satisfaction and the client paid and left. I took his place in the chair. As I settled in, an older man entered, walked to the back of the shop with a 'Bonjour' and sat down, picked up the paper and proceeded to read and comment on the news. The barber responded as he cut my hair. After a few minutes, the man stood up, said 'au revoir' and left. There was a moment's pause then the barber simply said, "He does that every day."

Summer is here. Julian's lavender is in full flower but there are not as many butterflies as in previous years. There have been few swallowtails, peacocks or silverwash fritillaries but Bath Whites are doing well.
The car parking fills up with walkers.
The 20yr old Charlène has produced her son, Milo, 3+kg. Grandfather Francis delighted.
La Dulcine continues to deliver the best lunch in Céret.
I've lost a bit of weight which should please my cardiologue.

It looks increasingly as though the Spanish Catalan second wave will result in the French re-closing the border. This has affected two planned visits. Mark is heading to Andalusia and has had to go by ferry to Bilbao, and Aidan who intends to drive from Madrid to Lausanne is now planning to cross through Galicia to avoid trouble in Catalonia.

Health report.
A few days ago I trapped a wasp between my left arm and belly. It stung me on the forearm. I googled what to do, washed with soap and warm water and applied an ice pack. Completely forgot to use the Aspivenin to aspirate the venom. Pain, swelling and inflammation ensued which I bravely endured. I socially distant consulted with Dr. McCullagh who advised lavender so I squirted some which we had purchased at the Lavender Farm and Museum in the Ardèche. It seemed to give temporary relief. After three days and lot of antihistamine tablets it has almost resolved. Everitt, not to be outdone, keeps exposing his bicycle injury abrasions, like a mediaeval beggar. He seems to be healing. I told him he should put sugar water on it to attract flies and sit on the floor outside Lidl, groaning. He'd make a packet.

Soon be time for a swim.

On Twitter: if you're refusing to wear mask due to concerns your brain won't get enough oxygen, I think that ship has already sailed.

Hope your summer is going well

Andrew

Hi-de-hi campers.

How is everyone? Enjoying the summer.

Summer has truly arrived. There have been some blistering hot days. Keith's pool temperature is 33+ which even Mrs Evans finds a bit too warm but it is delightful to go for a dip in the evening.

Intrepid Wendy has arrived. She flew in to Carcassonne and son Bass brought her to Balmanya, the property she and her late husband bought 50 years ago making her the Senior Brit in the haute Vallespir by a good few years. The house, actually three adjacent buildings, is further up the Route de Batère from us and down a 2k unmade track past the rural slum of the Rainbow camp. We drove Wendy up past the Gîte de Batère to the end of the tarmac and got out of the car to go for a walk. She was resplendent in her Beau (ed. Should it be Belle?) Geste outfit:

We set off up a steepish incline then off the main drag looking for an iron smelter she remembers from her youth. We must have taken the wrong path and were eventually halted by landslides and rock falls which was a relief to me. Embarrassing to be out walked by an 85yr. old lady.

We ate at the Gîte d'Étape restaurant. The food was simple but good and the view was spectacular. Our waiter spoke easy colloquial English having lived in Lancaster and Reading. (Why these two places we didn't establish, but they are both university towns.)

This is the weekend of the Fête de Léca. When we first arrived the Fête was held in Léca on the first Sunday in August. Several days before notices would appear under the windscreen wipers of cars parked on the Place warning if imminent grass cutting with the Fête to follow. The grass was cut, tables, chairs and great canvas marquees were delivered. On Sunday morning an alter was erected and ranks of chairs assembled facing the alter- and our balcony. People arrived mainly from Corsavy, cars were parked everywhere, hands were shaken, cheeks were air kissed. The priest arrived, put on his long white robe and conducted the mass. Afterwards everyone shook hands and kissed those they had missed and aperitifs were served. We would hide in the house, trying to keep the kids quiet till the service was over, then go down for the drink.

There were entertainments for the children. Franz's donkeys gave rides. A section of the river bed was dammed, barrels of trout were poured in and children tried to catch them with rod and line.

Later there was a communal meal at long tables under canvas followed by an entertainer. One year it was Eric el Català who played guitar and sang old Catalan songs that only a few older locals knew. Most of the audience were summer visitors, Parisians staying in their grandfathers house in Corsavy who spoke about as much Catalan as me.

About 15-20 years ago the day of the Fête was very hot, un vrai canicule. During the meal much wine was drunk. A man in his 80s passed out. The cry went up, "Esqu'il-y-a un Medicin dans la maison?" Or something of that sort. To which the answer was, "Oui, il-y-a un medicin anglais. Malheureusement il est pédiatre mais tant pis." So i became Physician General to the Fête and found myself, a recently appointed consultant paediatrician, ministering to a drunk 80yr. old French man with thermal stress. I got him laid flat in cool shade, he was conscious, gave him water and suggested he needed a wee rest. This was not dramatic enough for someone who decided to call the Sappeurs Pompiers. They duly arrived and decided to take him to hospital. They wrapped him in a Silver foil space blanket. This is a technique used for preserving heat in patients in shock, or following cold stress. I can't imagine what his temperature rose to as he cooked in his space blanket on his way to hospital. Apparently he survived.

After this event, the mairie decided that it wasn't safe to have the Fête in Léca and it was transferred to Corsavy.

One year in Corsavy a scratch band got together to play. They practiced in Fred's Shed. Our son Simon became lead singer because he could sing, classically trained, and he knew all the words to the songs of The Red Hot Chilli Peppers. And who of us could hum one of their greatest hits?

Two years ago newcomer Laure decided to re-establish the Fête de Léca in Léca. A committee was formed of young enthusiastic newcomers. And Mme. Bosch. A meeting was held, suggestions were made, donkey rides, fishing, climbing, running, jumping, standing on one leg, breathing in....to each of which Mme. B sucked in her breath, shook her head and muttered darkly about health and safety, and Commune insurance. But they went ahead wit a whole day event last year culminating in an evening bbq with musc and dancing long in to the night.

This year the format was changed to a Saturday evening bbq for the residents and the Sunday morning mass followed by a bbq lunch and children's activities.

Saturday morning arrived hot and muggy. Laure messaged to say that rain was expected at 18.00 for one hour after we would be able to proceed. She wasn't wrong. Through the late afternoon dark clouds appeared and at six o'clock a violent electric storm arrived. And hail. Not the hail we get in Southern England with stones the size of grains of rice. Golf balls. Tennis balls. Crashing on the roof, drumming on the velux skylight, exploding on the balcony.

And after an hour it stopped. And the evening went ahead. Lots of chicken and sausage on the bbq and bowls of salads. And wine.

Music provided by Nico Llory (see L'Homme Parle on YouTube) with his laptop and sound system.

The next morning I went to examine the car which was parked under trees. It was covered with leaf debris shredded off the trees by the hail. As I cleared it off it became apparent that the roof and bonnet were peppered with small dimples. And the windscreen looked as though it had been shot with an elephant gun.

Have a good summer

Andrew

Pubic hair beer   11/08/20

Bonjour.

On 4 Aug we celebrated Wendy, 85y old and 50y in the valley. The mayor (Antoine) came. He first met Wendy when he was a 19yr old hippy squatting at Vilalte. He and Ed entertained us with their very different violin styles. Then Antoine produced his mandolin. It's always amazing to see this giant of a man with his huge hands and big muscular forearms picking out a tune on a little mandolin.

Walking to the tower at Batère. In the spring there are thousands of fat tadpoles in the puddles. Where do all the frogs go?

Driving down to Corsavy on our way to lunch the other day we passed a large camper van parked in a pool of sunshine in a lay-by. At the back of the van was what appeared to be a rather lumpy leather ottoman. Further inspection revealed that the ottoman was wearing a piratical head scarf and sunglasses. It was in fact not an ottoman at all but a female of a certain age on a sunbed, topless, working on her tan, though as she seemed to be made of mahogany coloured leather it was difficult to imagine what more her melanocytes had to offer.

A Canadian brewery has been selling a beer which they called 'Huruhuru', which they believed to be a Maori word meaning feather. It turns out that it actually means pubic hair. They have been accused of cultural appropriation by a maori media person. They have, of course, apologised and are rebranding the beer. Shame. "Two pints of pubic hair please barman, and some pork scratchings."

Rural life.

Leaving the house the other morning we happened upon our neighbour Bruno. He is a hunter and had been up the mountain at dawn with a friend. They were attempting to stuff a dead chevreuil into a cold box preparatory to driving back to Nîmes. Not something you see in Beckenham.

Watched the first Test Match against Pakistan. Very exciting. Looked as though we were toast then Woakes and Buttler saved the day!

Don't forget your Factor 50.

Andrew

Cow Parsley   16/08/20

Greetings.

Well, things don't seem to be going so well. Numbers of new cases going rapidly upwards in the UK, France, Spain....and Australia, or West Island as John Warren has got me calling it (for those who don't know John, he's a Kiwi.). There have been cases in Céret and Amélie- probably tourists here for the 'cure'- ha! No cases in Léca yet. Those of you planning to come out in September/October, what are you thinking now? Hope we'll still be seeing some of you.

We've been walking a bit. The thistles at Batère are gorgeous

There has been no attention to the track to the tower at Batère and in places it is becoming narrower as the brambles, broom and bracken encroach making it a more and more enjoyable walk. Wild strawberries if you look carefully. There are few people up there so it's almost as though we have it to ourselves. The blackberry harvest looks promising.

Walking in the hills just across the river Têch from Arles we saw indigo coloured sloes ripening, hazelnuts, rosehips, lots of bright green prickly chestnuts.

When we first came to Léca the meadows and hillsides were grazed by Jaques Boher's sheep which he moved around the land with his dogs. It wasn't unusual when walking down the lane, to hear a whistle, a sharply spoken command or a bark, looking up you saw Jaques herding a troop of leggy tough mountain sheep along the side of an impossibly steep slope.

Jaques retired and the herd was taken over by Franz who lacked the necessary skills. The herd were left to their own devices and were eventually sold and Franz took to the road. So now the land is not grazed, the bracken, gorse and brambles are thick on the hillsides and the meadows are knee high with grass and flowers- clover, hawksbeard, many others and masses of white flowers of thin stemmed cow parsley. The grass is turning yellow in the summer heat. I worry about fire.

Cow parsley is edible, or, as Wikipedia has it, 'considered to be edible'. A sharp flavour with a hint of carrot. But before you start putting it in your salad be aware that you need to be able to distinguish it from it's close relation hemlock. Socrates was condemned to death in what we would now call a show trial with ludicrous charges. He was obliged to take a drink made of hemlock. (Ed. Don't try this at home.)

Talking of food that is supposed to be edible, Robert Macfarlane in his book, The Old Ways, described a trip to Bass Rock to collect fledging gannets. He asked his guide what they tasted like. "Well, my dog ate one once, then spent the next week licking his arse to get rid of the taste."

What's the most disgusting food you've ever had? I think mine was a Spanish specialty, a stew which I think was veal brains, tripe and liver. (Wally, you were there). Then there's andouillette which has nothing to commend it. And once in a Café in Piraeus at dawn with a breaking hangover I was induced to consume a soup which appeared to consist of lumps of discarded fish fat floating in oily grey warm water.

Bon ap, Andrew

Apocalyptic scene   17/08/20

Having sent out the last edition yesterday we went for a walk this morning. It's as if the Commune are seeing my emails and are bent on spoiling my fun.
There were 9 vehicles at the parking with walkers setting off in every direction.
But more upsettingly, the verges have been cut back. I say 'cut'. Some monster caterpillar-tracked vehicle has been through, slashing, ripping, destroying, leaving an apocalyptic scene of ravaged nature.

There is an odour of decaying vegetation mixed with a pleasanter smell of pine. The track is littered with the plant remains. All the roadside pleasures, blackberries, wild strawberries, flowers, have gone. The flies, rendered homeless, are out in force.
It will, of course, grow back and heal but it seems a very destructive and thoughtless bit of maintenance.

Best wishes
Andrew

The Butcher's back!   21/08/20

So, Biden and Harris have the Democratic Ticket. I can only wish them well. It is extraordinarily, reading social media, how many Americans seem to think 'Socialism' is some sort of evil demonic plot to take over the world, and anyone who doesn't support Trump wants to inflict socialism on God's Own US of A. Perhaps they don't believe that a civilised society should look after those less fortunate or less able. To some, Biden/Harris will drag the USA into a socialist hell and that will be the end of democracy.

More importantly, Corsavy has been in the National News (France 3). There is apparently pressure on the mobile phone companies to improve coverage nationally- which means essentially rural areas. Bouygues approached our Mairie with a proposal to place a 4G mast next to the old Corsavy signal tower, which I have to say is an interesting conjunction of old and new aids to communication. The local residents reacted with inevitable French outrage to this unconsulted 'decision'. A slogan was painted in red on the wall at the entrance to the village, and was promptly over painted with a contrary slogan in blue. A committee was formed and a petition launched. To be fair, they are not against the mast, just the site, pointing out, amongst other things, that it wouldn't cover Léca. We are obviously supportive of this objection. We have no mobile coverage in Léca so delivery drivers can't all us. Then there are those moments when you are trying to do something with the bank and they send an SMS with a code and we have to jump in the car and drive down to Corsavy to pick up the SMS before it expires in 15mins..
A second site has been proposed, 500m further away, close to a large electricity pylon.
There are those who object to the defilement of the view, and apparently those who object to the pylon being sited on land belonging to an unpopular farmer who would benefit from the rental charge. The petition has 130 signatures which doesn't seem much but does represent about two thirds of the population. I wonder what Trump supporters would make of this democracy in action.

It's all rather reminiscent of the time 13 years ago when France wanted to sell electricity to Spain. The plan was to construct pylons carrying high tension cables past Corsavy and over the border. The objectors raised all manner of reasons why the THT should not come our way- it caused cancer, abortions, haemorrhoids (ed. That's not true.) etc. And eventually the cable went under the sea so presumably the fish are suffering the consequences.

I'm thinking of getting a red baseball cap with MAGA on it. That's Make Arles-sur-Têch Great Again.

Breaking News
D D D DDD D D D DDD D D D DDD
(Ed. That's the teletype machine chattering. Jimmy Stewart will come in with a trilby on the back of his head and read the message...)
The Butcher of Arles has done it again! Once again he has stabbed himself!! Not so seriously this time. The blade went through his apron, jacket and shirt. And superficially cut the skin of his belly. He seems to have survived. We are now rather anxious about having ordered a deboned leg of lamb for Sunday lunch.

Our buddleia is now in full bloom. The French call it arbre papillon and, sure enough, it is now alive with butterflies- silver wash fritillary, swallow tails, hummingbird hawk moths.
Sitting on the balcony reading a book, I am amazed by the wonders of nature. Suddenly a tiny black dot appears on the paper and starts to move across the text. This insect, smaller than a full stop, has three pairs of articulated legs, head, thorax, abdomen, mouth parts, antennae and the rest. Amazing.

Whilst it may not be true that wine keeps Covid away, I'm up for testing the theory.

Cheers

Andrew

Brown feet   25/08/20

Stop press: I'm pleased to report that Roger has survived his latest self inflicted wound and provided us with a spectacularly good boned leg of lamb which Mrs. Evans stuffed and roasted to perfection.

Since the end of March I have worn socks on only two occasions when wearing trainers for walking. Otherwise I am barefoot or in sandals. As a result I have brown feet, which is nice. However I noticed this morning that my feet are turning into the feet of a lizard with shiny scaly wrinkled skin. David Icke would approve.
Some of you may not be familiar with Mr. Icke. He was Hereford United goal keeper before becoming a professional conspiracy theorist which seems to have provided him with a good living. Amongst other things he believes that a race of shape shifting reptilian aliens with evil intent are seeking to control and subdue the world. Apparently our own dear Queen is one of the reptile illuminati. And judging by the state of my feet, I'll be joining her soon. I wonder if Trump has heard about Icke. I'd have thought he's a hot candidate for Security Advisor.

Mas Cazenove, Tony and Lucy's Place, is currently occupied by their son Ed who decided some weeks ago that it was more enjoyable during lockdown to be in the Vallespir than in South London. He is a professional violinist so that most of his work has dried up and all he has left is teaching young children which he does on line. His broadband isn't working so he comes to us and does his class on his laptop in our kitchen. There is something charming and slightly surreal hearing snatches of classical music as he warms up, then the lesson starts. Ed plays a demonstration few bars then Hector, aged 8, wicked haircut, scratches out a dire facsimile which Ed praises, and so the lesson progresses. Hector is lucky to have such a patient encouraging teacher.

Lunch today at La Dulcine with Jonathan and Sue. Usual high standard, enhanced by being the only customers, good for us, not so good for them. Jonathan introduced me to a new phrase which I felt deserved wider exposure. He described a friend who worked in the French airline industry as having his 'bum in the butter'. This was in reference to the perks of his job which included seriously cut price flights enabling him to fly around the world.

Our next door neighbour has a 'Femtocel'. I know, I know, it sounds like something rather intimate for ladies but is in fact a device for enabling mobile phones to work through the internet where there is no mobile service. Clever. We have acquired a French SIM card and fired up an old iPhone so that by using Michèle's Femtocel we have mobile connectivity in Léca. I have no idea how this was achieved. You'll have to ask the wife.

So as you can tell, life continues at a gentle pace in Léca.

Hope all's well in your world.

Andrew

Arles Cockrell Saga   28/08/20

International news.
Best news of the week, nay the year, the decade.
Wild poliomyelitis has been eradicated from Africa.
It can now only be found in Afghanistan and Pakistan.
I can remember in the fifties being taken to the GP for polio immunisation. My memory is of a big syringe - glass and stainless steel, blunt metal needle, all cleaned, autoclaved if you're lucky, and re-used hundreds of times- containing a large amount of pink liquid which was injected into my arm. Pain!
I can remember, as a child, going to see Danny Kaye in 'The Five Pennies' , he played Red Nichols whose daughter contracted polio and was treated in an iron lung. Imagine the terror.
I can remember seeing kids at school with a withered leg in a heavy caliper of steel rods and leather straps, from hip to ankle articulating with an orthopaedic boot which had a thick platform sole to compensate for the leg shortening
I can remember in the mid '70s working in Zambia and seeing the long term survivors of the '50s epidemic which started in Africa and swept north into Europe and across the pond. Adults with deformed wasted legs sitting on wheeled trolleys begging in the street.
I can remember working at Queen Mary's Hospital, Carshalton in the late '70s. An old hospital with mixed paediatric wards, originally a Fever Hospital. In the '50s polio epidemic it had wards full of children in iron lungs. Check out photos from Picture Post on the Internet.
And now polio has been eradicated from Africa. And thanks largely to the monumental efforts of the WHO- Donald Trump please note. We should celebrate.

But still you get these fucking antivaxers propagating their lies about vaccines.

Rant over.

Regional news.

You may have seen in the news that topless sunbathing caused a stir.
At St. Marie la Mer, just down the road, a family complained to police that three topless sunbathers were 'upsetting' the children. The police asked the topless ones to cover up. Furore ensued. Politicians made statements, the hapless police were censured. It was established that , subject to local bylaws, topless sunbathing is the

god given right of every French woman. And man I guess.

Data was produced. Women were surveyed and asked if they ever went topless. 22% of French women said yes, 34% of German women, and a staggering 48% of Spanish women. I guess that's what happens when a country is released from decades of puritanical dictatorship. Look out North Korea. And what's going to happen when the SNP get thrown out of Scotland?

Local news.

The Saga of the Arles Cockerel.

As you drive up through Arles you pass rows of town houses on the right with the occasional ginnel going up steps to the back. Behind are large gardens and allotments. And some new houses.

One plot is owned by a woman who lives elsewhere but keeps chickens on her land. And a cockerel. The cockerel starts to regale the neighbourhood at about 4am. Some of the neighbours find this disturbs their sleep. Eventually one of the neighbours in a new house at the back took her to court. And won. An injunction was placed on the cockerel.

The woman appealed. And won. On the basis that the land was farm land before the new housing went up so keeping chickens was traditional usage.

Neighbours can be shits, can't they?

Our neighbours have chickens. When asked if they would be getting a cockerel, Laure replied, "No, I like my neighbours too much."

Chickens are great recyclers. We feed them most of our food waste. We have to remember to crush the egg shells so they don't learn to eat eggs. We obviously don't give them chicken bones which would be weird, or citrus, but there is debate about potato peel. They're very keen on rice and sweet corn husks.

Walking up the hill this morning, blackberries are ripening, sunflowers in gardens have developed huge flat seed heads. Now the temperature has dropped and the rain has come. Autumn.

Just looked on Twitter for an amusing sign off, but it's all spite and general nastiness. But. There is a thread beginning to trend about Jewish women who went (or were sent) on dates with Jared Kushner in his youth. Potential hilarity there. And his father was in and out of jail. He couldn't find an NJG and had to make do with a convert.

Happy fruit picking

Andrew

With some nudity

02/09/20

Patricia.

About a week ago Linda was out walking when she met Patricia.

She is one of three ladies of a certain age in Léca who look much the same, quite tall, spectrally thin, gaunt, with lined leathery faces. That scene from Macbeth comes to mind except you never see them together round a cooking pot clutching eyes of newt.

What we knew about Patricia was that she appeared in Léca about 10 years ago as a lodger at Can Robert with Franz the useless shepherd and Bettina his mate. The story was that Franz developed a passion for Patricia who in turn developed a passion for Bettina. This was clearly a bit tricky and Bettina left. After awhile Franz sold his sheep and donkeys and did something unique in my experience, he chose to become a tramp and headed off down the road. He said he wanted to explore France. He is now, I believe, shacked up with a woman in Cahors. So Patricia found herself living alone in Can Robert.

Linda and Patricia fell to walking together and chatting. She spent her first 20 years In Paris and two years in London doing some sort of course run by Cambridge University. I believe she was then a teacher but we don't yet know how she washed up in Léca.

She's work in progress.

Weather report

Just after my last diary we had a night of heavy rain, continuing for much of the following day. The next day there was snow on Canigou. In August! Twenty four hours later it had all gone.

Oysters

Yesterday Nigel, Ian and I made a pilgrimage to the oyster shacks on the Étang de Leucate. We journeyed in the McCullagh Duster (Pronounced 'Doo-stair'), thanks Tony, returning after a dozen moyenne each and a dozen prawns to share, washed down with a little Picpoul de Pinet, via the site of the Battle of Le Boulou. This action took place just after the revolution when France was in turmoil and Spain thought they could grab Catalonia Nord. They were mistaken.

TV Journalism.

One of my irritations is that thing where a sensitive topic is being aired and some poor victim is introduced "We spoke to Doris (or Louise, Michael, Farah, Sammy.....),

Page | 72

which is not her/his real name....". Why is it necessary to give them a name?

Lidl's Wine Fair.
Once a year, Lidl hold a wine fair when they sell lots of seemingly half decent wine at knockdown prices. We were invited by friends for a wine tasting. We arrived at Lidl at 08.45 this morning, went into the store to buy a bottle of the three wines we had identified and headed out to the car park where we joined four other couples at the back of David's truck which had become a bar and proceeded to taste the wines. I can't claim to have tasted all 15 bottles, not keen on warm white wine, after red, at 9o'clock in the morning. We then headed back to the store to buy the ones we liked. When we got home I had a little zizz. Indeed Mrs. Evans is snoozing on the settee whilst I write.

Nudity.
There you are, your patience is rewarded.
There has been a dramatic spike in Covid cases at Cap d'Agde centered in a nudist camp of 800 people who favour sex shows, writhing around in huge foam baths and doing something called 'swinging'. Well, I don't understand, I used to enjoy going on the swing in the park when I was a child but I don't remember ever catching anything.
Apparently 30% of them have tested positive. Some people live in these places permanently. Ain't that weird?

It's autumn. Something is eating the tops off our parsley.
Happy lockdown

Andrew

Patricia (continued).

Walking up the track past Can Robert, towards the headwaters of our river at the place called Le Faig, pronounced 'fatch', there are three properties each with its own drive. The first is to the right to La Casasse, the second is to the left down to Mas de Léca, the third is very short to La Tourre d'en Glas. All three are owned by the Firenzen family who are owners of a pharmaceutical company in East Germany. The matriarch recently died so that the three children have inherited.

We first went to La Casasse on our first visit to Léca after we had bought the house. Jane and Ewan Keane had been staying in the house and were supposed to leave the key when they decamped to La Casasse. We arrived after dark, by car with three tired sons and my mother. Door locked. No key. We eventually found our way to La Casasse. The door was unlocked, the remains of a fire was smouldering in the grate, a bottle of wine lay on its side, the dregs spilled out. We knocked, we entered, we shouted. Nothing. We put the children down to sleep and tucked my unimpressed mother up in an easy chair. It was close to midnight. I went for a little explore down a corridor, opening doors. The first two were locked. The third opened. A huge dog reared up at me in a somewhat aggressive manner. A torch came on. On a mattress on the floor were Jane, Ewan and two children. They had slept through our shouts. The house is now occupied by a man called Michèl whose partner left some years ago.

Mas de Léca is an old farmhouse with an enormous grange attached. Many years ago an English couple rented it. They wanted to buy it but it was very gloomy inside with thick walls, small rooms and tiny windows. They could not obtain permission to make the necessary changes and left. There have been no permanent occupants since. The owners have put it on the market with 55 hectares for 200,000€. Anyone interested?

La Tourre is now little more than a ruin of what was once a substantial property. Those of you who have been paying attention will recall that we have walked to it several times in spring. There were signs of occupancy but we never saw anyone. Apparently, according to Patricia, The Firenzens hired a man called Fabien to do work including making good the awful unmade road. They gave him 1500€ and he promptly took off for a holiday in the Canaries. Now he's back, living in La Tourre and driving his monster road flattening machine up and down. Patricia says he is a nasty violent man and Michèl is terrified of him.

We went to Intermarché on Friday to stock up. Now I have insight, self knowledge, I am aware that I am a bit overweight (less than I was though, cardiologue please note.) but honestly, I think it must have been National Morbid Obesity Day. Vast people everywhere, one with a tracheostomy, another with acanthosis nigricans, using trolleys like Zimmer frames, buying ready meals, biscuits and crisps. And Coca Cola. Stocking up for the weekend. Made me feel relatively slim.

For many years I have seen what I have always assumed were beetles in flight, often exploring holes on the lintel and door frame, sometimes entering the living room. They are big beast with black head, thorax and abdomen and wings which are dark brown but with a lovely violet or blue sheen. I now learn that they are solitary bees, Carpenter Bees, who seek rotten tree trunks to burrow into where they lay their eggs. Though they are an impressive size, they are not aggressive and rarely sting.

Went to Els Simiots last night for dinner. We ate there on the Saturday lunchtime of our 40th wedding anniversary weekend. Richard and Delphine subsequently sold the business and it is not anything like as good. Disappointing. Thank goodness for La Dulcine.

Guests arriving so must sign off.
Toddle pip

Andrew

Correction

Fabien was paid 15000€ by the Firenzens and took off to Beefa (ed. Surely that's Eye-beefa in the Bally Ariks). He wouldn't have had much of a holiday on 1500€?
And the sign off should be 'Toodle-pip' which I acquired from Dr. McCullagh. Otherwise all correct.

Enjoy your day,
A

Foolish Yellow toads   11/09/20

Chestnuts roasting on the open fire.....

Diana Rigg has died! She was only 82 which for some of us suddenly seems no age at all.

I saw her once in Merchant of Venice at Stratford when I was at school. Peter O'Toole was Shylock. I then met her in the 80s as a private consultant paediatrician. Her daughter had asthma and she wanted to discuss where they were living on one of the busiest rat runs in west London and whether it as a contributing factor. The answer was 'Yes'. Michael Parkinson thought she was the sexiest woman on the planet. Can't say I agree. Mind you, Parky never actually met my wife.

Autumn is coming. Keith's pool is cooling down. 27deg yesterday. Lots of hazelnuts. Apples for sale at the roadside. Crabapples scattered across the road between Corsavy and Léca. Chestnuts are beginning to fall in the wind. They are tricky devils, balls of sharp, sharp spikes, then small brown nuts. And how do you deal with them? They're impossible to peel. Do you cut them, boil them then peel them? Impossible. My advice, buy them in jars from Intermarché. But there will be hundreds of people out gathering them.

Driving back from dinner in Oms after a storm we saw lots of yellow toads sitting foolishly in the road.

We have history with toads. Several years ago we drove from Sydney to Adelaide and took the train, the Gann, to Darwin. We then went on safari in the Kakadoo National Park. We were told we would be 'glamping'. We imagined large tents with easy chairs, a table and chairs in the porch and a Sepoy serving Gin & Tonics before a delightful dinner. It wasn't like that.

It was end of season, we were the only guests, Max, our driver/guide was the cook in the rather grim mess tent, our tent was a rather grubby affair, camp beds, sleeping bags, 'clean' liners provided. The 'facilities' were about 50 yards away. Mrs Evans set off to the toilet block in the dark. A large creature ran across her foot. In the shower as she began her ablutions a Cane Toad the size of a football came waddling under the door to join her. Not happy.

We never have to buy bay leaves. Every spring our neighbour, Gerard, comes down from Toulouse and hacks back his garden. We arrive home to find a huge sprig of fresh cut bay hanging on our door handle. This goes onto the hook under the stairs for 6 months to dry and then, last Tuesday I took it down, stripped the leaves and put them in jars.

Our Department, Pyrenees Orientales, has been a red zone this week, numbers of C19 cases shooting up in France, Spain and the U.K. We have, with enormous regret, cancelled our planned trip to Switzerland. We are going ahead with a week in Torredembarra so long as the border remains open. Return to the UK at the end of November remains hopeful but Australia on Christmas Eve seems increasingly unlikely.

We had another broadband outage this week. The phone cables come up the hill from Arles sur Têch following the road and weaving their way amongst the branches of the dense roadside trees. When there are storms, trees fall, branches break off, and phone cables are broken. Unfortunately, the guys who are responsible for fixing the phone lines are not responsible for fixing the trees, and the guys who are responsible for fixing the trees are not in the least bit interested in the phone lines. Consequently, no one seems to think it would be a good idea to pre-emptively clear the branches from the cables, and to remove the dead trees balanced precariously above phone lines for months before they come crashing down, usually in the middle of stormy weather when multiple line breaches have occurred. But, this time it was different. The mountainsides around Léca are a source of timber. Loggers go up the forestry tracks and cut down timber which is loaded onto enormous trucks, usually Spanish, which then wend their way down the narrow winding mountain roads, always fun if you meet one coming the other way. One such truck managed to snag a phone cable as it took a corner between Corsavy and Arles, cutting all phone connection up the valley. This wasn't deemed urgent, so was fixed the next day.

Walked up to Mas Cazenove today to go scrumping. Lots of apples and some rhubarb. Took the duster back to have the windscreen replaced. Parked it in Léca. Mrs E. in an awful tizz because couldn't find evidence of current insurance. Worried that we had driven and parked on the public highway. I spent some time trying to remember when I had last seen a gendarme going round the parking in Léca checking vehicles. When I say 'some time' I mean about 3 nanoseconds. And bear in mind, at least half of the vehicles parked here are short of documentation. Greatly relieved to hear from Mrs McCullagh that the vehicle is in fact insured. Did you ever doubt it?

Had lunch at Chéz Françoise with the Everitts and the Sims. Drink was taken. JS regaled us with a tale which made us roar with laughter, but I have decided that it is too obscene for this diary. But if pressed, I may be persuaded....

Stick to groups of six.
There was a great buildup to a new French announcement this afternoon, but the Prime Minister seems to have basically said, "Mind how you go." No new measures introduced.

Tinkety tonk (continuing the Dr. McCullagh-speak theme.)

Andrew

In my last offering I mentioned the Gann. My current carer has pointed out the spelling error. The train is called The Ghan. In the early days of opening up Australia the city of Darwin on the north coast was about as far away from the main centres (Melbourne, Sydney, Adelaide and Brisbane) as was possible, separated from these cities by The Red Centre, an arid wasteland of ancient rock and desert. Communication and trade was necessary. The Australians realised that the best way to cross the Red Centre was by camel so they imported camels and their drovers from Afghanistan and these animals and their human drovers carried goods and mail between Darwin and Adelaide. Then the railroad was built and the camels were redundant. The drovers were told to kill their animals. They were unable to do this to their beloved animals and released them into the wild. This history is memorialised by the Ghan, a tourist train which takes you on a three day journey across the desolate centre of Australia. In 2008 the feral camel population was about 1million. Australia has exported racing camels to Saudi Arabia. There has been a cull and the population has fallen. I was disappointed that during our trip we never saw a camel.

Keith has had a hornet's nest in his pool pump house. Now, I know some of you socialists are thinking "Second home, hornets, serves him right." But, hey, come on, he comes from Middlesbrough, lives in Manchester, was a successful teacher and is still contributing. He deserves his swimming pool. And he lets me use it. The original report suggested Asian hornets, but in fact they were European hornets which are larger with yellow abdomens whereas the Asian are mostly black with yellow faces and lower legs. President Trump would probably call them China Hornets if they were brought to his attention. As the Americans do bigger and better, it is apposite that the Asiatic Giant Hornet appeared in Washington State in 2019. The Asian/yellow legged hornet came to the U.K. in 2016 but is confined to the south because they cannot tolerate the cold northern winters. The nest was huge and has to be disposed of because the pupae will rot and stink. The hornet man suggested chucking it over the fence into the neighbour's land. Seems a bit harsh.

Keith has a Chinese barbecue. It's a cast iron pot which he bought in a garden centre in Stockport over 20 years ago for £6.50. Bargain I say. Suggested he try putting it on Antiques Roadshow.

OK, he can only cook two steaks at a time, but it's a work of art.

Went to Banyuls beach today. Sadly the Centre Héliomarin convalescent facility is being pulled down and rebuilt as an old people's home. I joined the watercolour group for my first attempt at painting for six months. The results were terrible. Linda went snorkelling and topped up her tan.

We got a Facebook notification saying that the Spanish border was to be closed on Friday. This turned out to be 'fake news' based on a false report in a Spanish media outlet six weeks ago.

People are being attacked by biting fish in the Mediterranean. The fish in question is the trigger fish, an ugly bugger which reminds me of Peter Hitchins. Is that libel, or slander?It's just an opinion. This strengthens my reluctance to venture into the sea.

*** If you are easily offended by smut, please stop reading now.***

I have been persuaded that I should give you the story which JS regaled us with. So here it is. I have embellished it a little. I hope that's ok Jon.

A woman of a certain age was admitted to Intensive Care. She was unconscious. Over time she was stabilised and no longer required ventilation. But she didn't wake up.

A nurse gave her a bedbath and noticed that when she washed he ladyparts the woman stired and her breathing pattern changed. She reported this to the consultant.

He consultant gave this some thought and then spoke to the husband. He suggested, somewhat awkwardly, that, in an effort to wake his wife up, he should try cunilingus. The husband, in reply, says that he never did latin at school and doesn't understand what the consultant is suggesting.

So the consultant says, "Oral sex. Try oral sex. That might do the trick."

So the man goes into his wife's room, the curtains are drawn, the door is shut. The consultant and the nurse wait expectantly outside.

Ten minutes later the husband burst out of the room, his clothing in disarray.

"Did it work?" cried the consultant.

"I'm not sure," replied the husband, "but she nearly choked!"

Remember the rule of six. Which doesn't apply in France.

Best wishes

Andrew

Good morning (Good evening antipodeans)

Windy yesterday, rain this morning, leaves turning, lots of cars parked along the road as fungus hunters go to work.

A few days ago we noticed that the shutters of the Fargue house opposite were open. Gerard and Antoinette had left about a week ago. Then we remembered that his 20yr old grandson, whom we have known from early childhood, was due to come with his girlfriend. After three days we have not seen nor heard anything of them. Do you think they're ok, should I pop over and knock? What do you advise?

I was rightly reprimanded by Keith for mistakenly saying he was from Middlesbrough. He is from the North East which to me as a 'Soft Southerner' means Newcastle (which I obviously pronounce 'New-Car-sl'), Middlesbrough, Wallsend and Lindisfarne.

I went to Newcastle first aged 16 for an interview for medical school. Indeed, I would have gone there if Edinburgh hadn't sufficiently lowered their sights that I was able to scrape in.

I've been in court in Newcastle and Middlesbrough as an expert witness. I found the latter a depressing down at heel place in need of investment.

I've never been to Wallsend, so named because of Hadrians Wall, which I once had an ambition to walk along. Don't think my knees would permit that now. I daily expect Sturgeon to claim everything north of the wall as traditional Greater Scotland.

Never been to Lindisfarne. Great band though. One of my girlfriends was a fan and I bought her a Lindisfarne LP for her birthday. Still remember 'We can Swing Together'

I looked up the lyrics and was disappointed that it didn't include the lines, which I've heard them sing, ' We can swing together, we can have a wee wee, we can have a wet on the wall.'

BEARMAN.

It's the day of the Bearman Extreme Triathlon. I was going to enter but I've had this injury which has left me with a little niggle. I'm working hard with the Reiki, the cupping and Cranial Osteopathy, and am hopeful for next year.

There is a full triathlon and a half triathlon. There is a swim in the lake at St. Jean Pla de Corts, à bike ride and a run. The full version is a swim of 3.8km, bike ride 180km with 4700m elevation, and run 42km with 1475m elevation.

The half triathlon is 1.9km, 90km (1820m), 21km (800m). Andy and Fabien are doing this.

It's raining steadily, which is better than hot sun. But not much. I'm exhausted just writing this. I may have to lie down.

CÉPES

We never go fungus hunting. We did once pick a load of things which we thought were cépes. When we got back we showed our harvest to Antoinette Fargue. She laughed her head off and told us to throw them away. We've never tried again since.

Our neighbour, the amazingly fit, recently married, retired optician Claude, goes up the hill with a basket collecting various fungi with confidence. He's just given us a present.

That's just a small part of the bagful he gave us.

I'm going to have to google 'drying cépes' because we are going away tomorrow.

News Update

I'm happy to report that Thomas Fargue and his young lady have made an appearance without any prompting from me. They look strangely smug. What's that all about? Three days of strict self isolation can't be that much fun can it? Can it......?

Stay safe, stay well

Andrew

Spanish holiday: Finding Jesus   25/09/20

Hola.

But first, local news. Andy and Fabien finished their Half Bearman. Congratulations to them. This in spite of having to contend with a reported 2500 Spanish bikers who came over the border and followed a substantial part of the route- Arles, Corsavy, Batère, Montferrer. There was a lot of noise but remarkably no injury. As Keith pointed out, pre Schengen, the border posts would have been manned and this Tartar Horde would not have been allowed to pass.

The first two weeks of September loom large in the Evans Clan, with 4 birthdays, Sue, Lew, David and Nick. After that it's all downhill to Christmas. So off we went to PicWicToys in south Perpignan (other Toy outlets are probably available) to stock up on gifts for small people. So, that's Christmas shopping in mid September. The only problem is that even PicWicToys isn't yet in Christmas mode, so no paper with the requisite snowmen, Santa, robins, holly etc required to wrap presents for Australia, where, incidentally, Santa is likely to arrive in vest and shorts, on a surfboard pulled by kangaroos. I couldn't get used to Christmas dinner as a barbie on the beach. It's not right.

We arrived home from Perpignan to find three male Asian Hornets on our French windows (Porte fenêtre in French) so I dispatched them with a spray. Hope we haven't got a nest close.

And then I saw a mouse, where? There on the stair, right there, a little mouse with... well no, it didn't have clogs on and was in a bad way. (if you are puzzled at this point, check out ' A Windmill in old Amsterdam', Ronnie Hilton used to sing it. Should've got the Mercury Prize. It was a regular with Uncle MAC on Children's Favourites on the Light Program.) We think Michèle's cat must have brought the mouse in to play with. It was alive. Just. When you pick up a mouse by the tail it splays out its back legs and holds its front paws close, as if in prayer. Cute. Over the wall it went.

Spain.

So, ignoring advice from well meaning friends, we decided to come to Spain for a week. Numbers are going up in the UK. The impression I get is that it's all down to they students boozing and having sex, which is remarkable given how narrow and uncomfortable Halls of Residence beds are. Not to be outdone, the French numbers are worse. They were concentrated at holiday venues as the French nation went on their summer hols. Now they are returned home, distributing the virus to every corner of France. Except Léca. The Spanish figures are even worse. I don't know the explanation for this but I'm prepares to believe that students, sun and sangria are involved. And sex obviously.

So we drove to Roda de Berà near Tarragona to a house we stayed in last year. The owners departed over a week ago leaving keys in the key safe. The other properties round the communal pool are mostly owned by families from Barcelona who use them for main holidays and weekends. There were a few people here judging by cars, open shutters, lights on, but we saw nary a soul and by Monday afternoon they'd all gone.

The pool is a funny shape making swimming lengths a bit tricky, and the water temperature is bracing but we have had it to ourselves.

We walked down to the sea, wearing a mask (well, most of the time), and along the costal path. The people not wearing masks were the joggers and cyclists.

There are an awful lot of small pampered dogs around. Why, doggie people, do women with silly little dogs hold them up to their cheeks and take selfies with the sea in the background? What's that about?

How we found Jesus.

So, have you noticed how many people on the radio, when asked a question, begin the answer with So...

So, we decided to go to the Penedes in search of Cava, which some of you will know, is life blood, mother's milk to the present Mrs Evans. We set off to Sant Sadurni d'Anoia, the heart of the Cava industry. We decided to pass on the big familiar names and booked in to the Gramona Winery for their Sparkling Wine Tour. 20€ a head. In Spain it seems that you can't just turn up at a cellar door, taste some wine and buy as you can in France. In Spain you have to buy a ticket for a tour of the winery with a tasting at the end which can knock you back anything from 16-50€. I guess it's to stop busloads of tourists pitching up from the Costas, drinking and not buying.

We arrived at the winery, a large building next door to the Raventos Cave with numerous other caves , well known and little known, around the town. We were greeter by a flamboyantly loud lady who introduced us to our guide. We had found

Jesus. Well, actually, Jesús (pronounced Hay-zoos.). Named after his father, his grandfather,....We asked if he had a son. Yes, he has a son. Called Liam. He met his wife in Barcelona. She is from Shrewsbury

We spent over two hours with Jesús, hearing about the history of the business from its peasant farmer founder to major player in three generations. The fourth generation is now taking over, and two more are champing at the bit. We learned about how the wine is made, and how the Xarel.lo grape allows long aging in the bottle. Then we tasted the results. I have to say it's very good, as good, but different from, champagne. And some of it at champagne prices. We spent some money, shook Jesus by the hand and left.

That's all for now as I have to go and fetch Linda from the beach. Look out for Part 2, coming

soon.

Andrew

Spanish holiday part 2: The Priorat 27/09/20

Last year Richard Swarbreck proposed a trip to the Priorat to check out the wine. We weren't able to make it then, but finding ourselves only a gentle one hour drive away we decided to follow his recommendation. Looking on line, I found a list of the 'Ten Best Wineries of the Priorat'. I also had three recommendations from Jesús who used to work in the region, complete with contact names. I phoned Mas Doix and again came up against the requirement to buy a rather expensive two hour visit with a limited tasting at the end. And the wine was eye wateringly expensive.

So the I phoned Jesús' second choice. A man answered the phone, rattling off something in Spanish. I understood not a word, and said, "Hablas inglés?" - being spanish there should be an upside down question mark at the beginning but I can't find one on my iPad. "Yes." Came the reply. "Are you Paul?" "Yes." I was offered the standard wine tour, then the shortened version but I said I only really wanted to come, taste and buy. Paul said that was fine and to come at 3pm as he usually did a tour at 4pm.

The drive up next morning was delightful. We first drove to Poboleda where we stopped for coffee. We saw signs to several Caves but none for Mas Doix which seems to be playing hard to get. I couldn't find their location with certainty on the internet.

The man at the next table, having finished a large brandy, and whilst waiting for a beer, decided to have a chat. He was a man of indeterminate age, with a single central tombstone tooth in his upper jaw, surrounded by a tufty long ill kempt grey beard which I suspect he trimmed himself with hedge trimmers after a morning at the bar. He spoke first in French, then in English, keen to give us advice about our tour. We smiled and tried to ignore him.

On then to Escaladei, a beautiful place to go and taste some wine.

We first went out of the village to Cartoixa d'Escaladei. This is the ruins of a major monastery. King Alfons 1 having driven the Moors out of Catalunya, invited French Carthusian Monks from Grenoble to establish a monastery to reintroduce Christianity in the area. The monastery was established in 1194. The Prior became the effective overlord of the surrounding communities, hence Priorat. The monks introduced viticulture and wine making from Provence. All went well until the 19th cent. when the Spanish King, strapped for cash, closed the monasteries, and sold off their properties to private citizens. The local peasants, tired of oppression and servitude, pillaged the buildings and burnt them down, such was the affection with which the local populace held their religious masters. The estate was sold to a consortium of five families, two of whom are still in the business. History lesson over.

We returned to the Cellers de Scaladei. We were 45 min. early and a wine tour was coming to an end. Sales occurred, and sanitising of worktops and chairs took place. Then Paul introduced himself. Ex Leicestershire, ex Army Officer, ex Hospitality and Tourism graduate, ex husband, father, partner, oenology student. And in the mood to spend time with us.

A woman entered the Cave and engaged in a discussion with Paul in Spanish about possibly joining a tasting. Paul was clearly trying to fob her off. I said that we were happy to do a two language tasting. Paul shook his head and shushed me. After she bought a couple of bottles and left he explained that she was a Russian woman from the coast who comes about once a month, tries to drink the expensive wine and then buy the cheap ones.

We spent over two hours talking about and tasting 8 of their wines. This included a bottle of 57€ red which he opened with a device which removed the wine through needle and replaced the space with argon. Paul was enjoying himself at the end of the day, he explained that he did up to to 5 tours a day and normally spat into a bucket, so he was happy to sit and talk, and drink wine which he swallowed. So did we. We had a fantastic tasting which he completed with a tour of the winery. He told us that at the beginning of lockdown he had 180 bottles of wine in his own cellar. At the end he and his partner had reduced this to two bottles.

We bought some gorgeous wine. Not cheap.

This appeared on Facebook:

Jane and Arlene are outside their nursing home, having a drink and a smoke, when it starts to rain. Jane pulls out a condom, cuts off the end, puts it over her cigarette, and continues smoking.

Arlene: What in the hell is that?

Jane: A condom. This way my cigarette doesn't get wet.

Arlene: Where did you get it?

Jane: You can get them at any pharmacy.

The next day, Arlene hobbles herself into the local pharmacy and announces to the pharmacist that she wants a box of condoms.

The pharmacist, obviously embarrassed, looks at her kind of strangely (she is, after all, over 80 years of age), but very delicately asks what size, texture, brand of condom she prefers.

'Doesn't matter Sonny, as long as it fits on a Camel.'

The pharmacist fainted!

We've survived this long, I think we'll be ok. Andrew

Spanish holiday part 3: La Sort   30/09/20

It's clear that I don't proof read my diary adequately before pressing 'send'.
The bottle of wine that Paul gave the argon syringe treatment was 75€ and despite
his schmoozing we resisted buying. I really don't think my taste buds would
appreciate the subtlety of such an expensive wine, unless someone quite rich was
paying.
Also Paul is less of a reprobate than I alleged. His wine cellar was 120 bottles at the
start of lockdown, not 180. But if it had been 180 I suspect the result would have
been the same.

I described Keith as a son of Middlesbrough which he was quick to deny. He has
finally admitted to being from Doncaster, or 'the railway town' of Doncaster. Doesn't
make it better Keith.
I once took a train out of King's Cross to go to Middlesbrough to examine a child for a
court case. Just out of the station the train ground to a halt. There was 'something on
the line'. Well, it's a jumper, isn't it? We sat for about an hour. About half of the
passengers were, like me, aiming to change trains at Doncaster for the
Middlesbrough line. The train guard promised to phone ahead but warned that,
because it was a different company, he was unable to influence what would happen.
As we pulled in to Doncaster we watched the connecting train pulling out.
I took a taxi. The lawyers were paying. Proof, if need be, that there is something to
be said for a National Rail Service.

Spain.
We contemplated lunch at Cal Sisquet on the point at El Roc Sant Cayeta because we
fancied a paella, but we couldn't book and had to turn up and queue for a table.
Instead we decided to drive directly in land. We explored Bonastre, Masllorenç,
Castel de Rodonyà, Vila-Rodona where we stopped for coffee. Linda went in to the
pharmacy. There was a one way system. As she came to the exit, a very elderly lady
with a Zimmer frame came charging in, brushing her aside.
Then on to Santés Creus and finally El Pont d'Armentera where we parked up and set
off to find a restaurant. We were looking for the Restaurant La Sort. Using our
phones we set off through the winding streets eventually coming to a dead end. I
asked a man for directions. It turned out he was going to the restaurant. We
descended a stone stair and followed a track between stone walls and fences, finally
arriving at a gate with a sign- La Sort. The terrace was fully booked. We thought we
might eat at a table by the front door but it was too cold so we moved inside. We
were well spread out and enjoyed an excellent lunch. Snails followed by grilled lamb
for me, cannelloni then pork for Linda.
Returning to Léca on Sunday we saw what we had already learned on the internet

that there had been snow high up. Andorra and Les Angles were affected. The peaks of the Garrotxa, and the massif du Canigou were covered. When we got back to Léca it was cold. We broke out the hot water bottle. The leaves are on the turn, the chestnuts are falling, autumn has come.

On Monday there was an Emmeline Pankhurst Fan Club lunch at La Dulcine. Ten of us attended, including new recruit Robert and James who is far too young. Matters of moment were discussed and no serious conclusions were drawn. Which is as it should be. We sat outside and the sun favoured us. Don't think we'll be swimming much more.

I blame the students for wanting to have fun.

Andrew

Time to get serious   03/10/20

I feel that this diary has been getting a bit frivolous which is not entirely appropriate at this difficult time. Time to get serious.

In case anyone missed it, Donald 'Bonespurs' trump is in hospital with Covid. He has been treated with remdesivir and infused antibodies bled out of 'Antifa' menials kept in the basement for just this purpose. He hasn't, surprisingly, received hydroxychloroquin or intravenous dettol. My thoughts are with the virus.

Today there are more cases of Covid in the White House than there are in the whole of New Zealand.

On 30/09/20 new reported cases were Spain 11016, France 12845, UK 7108, with deaths 177, 63, 71 respectively.

In Spain there are no border restrictions and no quarantine for returning travelers, wear a mask out in public. The rule appears to be that, as most Spanish people do not breathe through their noses, the mask is worn below the nose. I presume that the many people who wear their masks even lower, covering chin and throat, are breathing through a tracheotomy. Though many of them are smoking. Antiviral cigarettes I expect.

France strongly advises against travel to Spain but doesn't prohibit it. The border remains open. Regulation has been devolved from the Élysée to local authorities. I'm told that the restrictions vary within Perpignan. Given that the mayor of Perpignan is National Front, I think we can all guess where that's going. Masks must be worn in shops etc and in street markets such as Céret Saturday market, and in restaurants till you are sitting down- when you cease to excrete the virus.

The UK requires self isolation for those returning from France and Spain. There is a degree of lockdown in the north of England though interestingly not in the Prime Minister's constituency where there have been similar numbers of deaths. If you are the PMs father you don't need to quarantine on returning from abroad and don't need to wear a mask in shops because if you're that posh you can't catch the virus. Then there's Scotland. The only one party state in Western Europe. If you're an SNP MP, and Covid positive, you can travel the length of Britain on public transport (twice) without getting sacked by your party because Wee Nicola, her with the wee tartan mask, is far too busy with her lawyers trying to obstruct the Salmond enquiry. In the meantime, in England, you can get married in a group of 15, and hold a funeral in a group of 30, but then break up into groups of 6 for the wake.

Keith seems to have occupied quite a lot of my time recently but now I have established that he hailed from the railway town of Darlington, on the Kings Cross to

York line. There is, of course, a town called Keith on the Elgin to Aberdeen road. I've been through Keith with Doug when we were visiting him in Forres. If memory serves, his father was the local vet..

Doug and I returned to North Scotland some years later for a painting holiday. We stayed in a hotel in Latheron which is on the east coast between Inverness and Wick. It was a strange establishment, old fashioned decor, high narrow squeaky beds, rooms impossibly small because of the insertion of an en-suite, which has to be just better than wandering down a draughty corridor in your dressing gown to queue outside the communal bathroom. The manager was a small man called Pedro who was from from Milton Keynes. He first tried to offer us rooms on the ground floor just off the main sitting area. He could see we were unimpressed and gave us rooms upstairs. We were disappointed to find that there was no Scottish beer on tap in the bar, and no local lamb, beef or seafood on the restaurant menu which was what you might call 'English International'. We expressed our dissatisfaction to Pedro who explained that the hotel was part of an English chain and the bar and the restaurant was the same in all their hotels.

Half way through the week, Pedro sidled up to me in the bar and asked me if I liked lobster. I responded to the affirmative. He said he would get some for Saturday.

On Saturday morning Pedro reappeared with a small plastic crate and asked, "will these be ok?" The crate contained several very small lobsters the size of langoustines, which is what you get in the cold waters of the North Sea. He then asked me how I want them cooked. I said that I would defer to the chef. So Pedro called the chef. Those of you familiar with Faulty Towers may remember McClunge, the huge, inarticulate, Scottish chef, wielding a cleaver. The chef was similar, though not holding a cleaver, and with a South Africa accent. He agreed with me that he knew what to do with them.

That evening we sat in the restaurant and were served the lobsters which were delicious. Many other guests, seeing this, and seeing that there was no lobster on the menu, asked if they could have the same. They were sadly disappointed. We retired to the bar feeling replete, and smug.

We stopped for bread at our favourite boulangerie on Thursday as we returned from the supermarket. The shop didn't have the 'pain céréales' which Linda favours, so she was offered bread with chorizo or olives or cheese. Now, I may be old fashioned, but I don't want stuff in my bread. If I want a chorizo sandwich I'll make one.

In other bread related news, I was well pleased to see that Subway, the American privately held franchise fast 'food' chain which primarily sells submarine sandwiches, has lost a legal case in Ireland. They had applied to reclaim VAT on their rolls because bread is VAT free in Ireland. They lost because for every 100g of flour in their rolls there is more than 10g of sugar, which in Irish law is not bread.

Gardening notes.
With autumn upon us, we have pulled up most of the bean plants which have given a good crop, and the carrots. There are a few late planted bean plants which have just started flowering, I doubt we'll get much out of them. The carrots were much too tightly packed and all we got were tiny, few more than an inch long, but nice and sweet. The potato plants grown from sprouting spuds abandoned by the bins at the campsite in Corsavy, have given us enough for a week's meals.
We have replaced them with some cabbage, cauliflower and celeriac. We are thinking of also trying winter spinach.
It's occupational therapy for the isolated elderly.

We saw Antoine, the sheep farmer, unloading bales of hay from an artic.. The hay is feed for the lactating ewes after lambing at the beginning of next year. It is special hay which was grown by the sea near Marseille and driven to Corsavy on a truck. I wonder if it produces the same result as feeding the animals on the salt flats of the Gower Peninsula, giving us the delicious 'Salt-Marsh Lamb'.

An older man was heading home down the motorway after a long day in the office, and a little after work refreshment, when his (hands free) phone rang.
Answering, he heard his wife sounding agitated. "Norman, I just heard on the news that there's a car going the wrong way on the M25. Please be careful."
"Hell's teeth, Doris," cried Norman, "It's not just one car, it's hundreds of them!"

Thank you Wendy.

Keep warm

Andrew